Inspiring Love

Jason Down

Bonker Books

Published by Bonker books
16 Gloucester Road
Milton Keynes
MK12 5DX

ISBN 978-0-9558184-1-7
Printed in the United Kingdom
By Bonker Books

www.bonkerbooks.com

A catalogue record for this book is available from the British library

Not wanting to grow up, torn between the inner child that lives in the realm of all possibilities, and adult hood. Slowly the inner spark was almost extinguished, until someone told me it's all an illusion.

Stepping on ones inner path is easy, holding to it is lonely and hard. This is a journey, a search for a personal truth, which would eventually lead me away from those stoned depressed days, allowing the Great Spirit that resides in us all to fly like an eagle. From Croatia and India to the mountains of Wales, my journey was one of the best. A family in tatters and friendships broken I discovered we learn the most through our pain, and laugh the loudest with each triumph as we overcome it. Never surrender, fight to the end and with love in our hearts, Dreams do come true as I have discovered.

Contents

Introduction

It has now been nine years since this period, in which I learned to believe in myself along with the universe. I wrote this book in the hope it may touch peoples lives in a positive way, that no matter how tough life becomes never surrender that spark of light. Having a dream and not knowing the path is part of life, making mistakes over and over is to walk that path. During this journey I was mentally full of doubt coupled with fear, but inside something drove me on not to listen to my overactive mind. That something was my heart the one true place I have learned, I can trust.

Chapter 1

Miserable

I made my way round to Dugs, it wasn't the best place to be right now, but I went anyway. Knocking I felt nervous. I was badly wounded and in need of a quick fix anything to take away the pain. It was over I'd lost my prize possession how could she leave me now. Hearing Dug near the door I felt nervous. "Hello mate come in." Dug was my oldest mate unstable in many ways, assured in others, but most of the time his social confidence was ever present in those shaky hands and constant red eyes. Aware that Nat would most likely be out back skinning up on Dugs gear I stepped into the hallway, unspoken I made my way down.

Dug and Nat were like rizzla and hash they complimented one another. Dug had an obsessive habit for long stints about certain friends while Nat enjoyed free lifts, free hash and Dugs constant approval. Entering the conservatory sure enough there was Nat.

"Alright big guy, how's it going?" I struggled to hide my shock and emptiness. Taking a few puffs his voice was muffled by the cloud of smoke leaving his mouth leaning forward he passed me the cone shaped joint. I toked hard on it before awkwardly announcing. "She's dumped me."

"Naa" Nat tried to sit up from his slumped position. "Yep, it's over." Realizing the bad buzz I had brought to Dugs back yard I quickly tried to remedy it. "I don't care, sod her anyway."

"Ah, but we know that you do care, and it has been coming." Dugs face was now aglow with delight at my down fall. "I mean you haven't got a lot to offer have you mate?" Realising I was on my knees I felt Dug was taking this opportunity to pay me back for what he saw as a lifetime of piss take and ridicule.

I was low naked without armour or little energy to defend myself. "You will have to sort yourself out mate, I've got a job, a car, and you know good things." Nat's input wasn't welcome what I really wanted to say was. "If it wasn't for your dad sorting you out every time you fucked up you'd be unemployed like me!" But deep down I knew I didn't mean it, Nat had always been a great friend to me.

I soon left Dugs, returning to the depressing atmosphere of the kitchen back home mine and Emma's parting argument still lingered. How could all that had been so good now be so shit, I loved her and my heart ached. Believing that my social life and friends mattered I thought I could live without her, what a fool. A mixture of sadness and depression swept over me. I felt cold and alone, a feeling that would haunt me for many years to come.

In the coming weeks the opportunity arose to move away and live with my brother and sister. In our own ways, life had hit us all hard, but we were strong. Mel my sister was the most generous person you could meet, 'heart of gold' I would all so often tell her, and I was without doubt her favourite of three. I saw through my sister's faults and drug habits, born seven years apart on the same day we had a very special bond. My brother Danny was my boyhood hero, what a character, the light and soul of any social gathering; yes, I wanted to be like him.

The house itself was a real shit ole, but as Mel pointed out it had potential. She would say. "Come Christmas it will be the bollocks." She was always positive about life but then I suppose she had to be. Before moving in I had insisted upon one thing, if brother Baz moved in, I was gone. I had enough going on in my own head without him complicating things. If you've ever been fishing, got your line in a tangle or a bird nest as we knew it, then he was the tangle. Only worse, it was at night, no torch with a big fish tugging on the end of your rod, just where, does one stop. He had no concept of truth or respect for people, or their belonging's he'd think nothing of selling your sentimental's for a pint and a packet of fags, despicable at times.

The weeks soon flew and my depression deepened no work, no money and no energy. I was surrounded by chaos the only blessing was I had plenty of company to distract me, as the house soon became a constant session of hash indulgence. Faces I'd known forever just kept coming and Jock was one of them. Knowing it was him at the door I let him in. "Hello mate, cup a rosy?"

"Lovely." Entering he took his usual seat. "Get one together shall I?"

"Course, avent been up long, wot's the time Jockey boy?"

"Just gone one" making into the lounge we joked about. "Put the telly on then." Going through to the kitchen I yawned. "Neighbours will be on soon."

"Hear you had a bit of a late one last night." Jock called out from the sofa.

"Yeah, Sam didn't leave till four, cell block H, Gladiators, Coach, it just rolls after midnight."

These rendezvous with Sam had become quite a regular occurrence his work shifts finished at eleven and he needed to unwind with a spliff or two.

The kettle finished boiling and I poured the tea. Carrying it into the front room I watched Jock light a large cone shaped joint up. "Coming out this weekend, boy?"

"I'm broke Jock times are hard." As I tried to hide it the embarrassment of my current situation silenced loomed. It must have been hard for Jock to understand where I was coming from, to me he had no concept of money, his family had done well during the eighties and he didn't go without. Despite his wealthy upbringing Jock always brought warmth to any session, very much like me he was a child who never grew up and whose innocence still showed. It wasn't long before the metre began sounding off. "Shit man, wos that bleeping?"

"Bollocks! It's the electric meter."

"And?" he quizzed.

"It means, there's only a quid left, then there's no more TV."

"Bit of a bad buzz, in it?"

"Tell me about it," accepting the cone I sighed. The smoke felt harsh, but left a good taste in my mouth. "Right son, I gotta shoot." Getting up Jock dug into his pocket and hand me all his loose change. "Get some electric cards, I'll ring ya later." I didn't move to see him out, just pulled hard on the joint, before dozing off in front of the box. Slamming doors and heated voices shook me from my slumber what seemed like some hours later, but the theme tune to Neighbours told me otherwise.

"Bollocks Mel! You said all I had to do was drive." I could hear Baz brushing down the hallway.

"And that's all I needed." Mel retaliated. I'd told Mel a thousand times, not to involve him.

"Alright Jay she said entering. "Look what I got, tiger prawns, and steaks! And some of that thousand Island, dressing you like."

"What's all that shouting about?" I asked.

"Oh, it's him, in it." Throwing Baz a scornful look Mel carried the shopping out back.

"I aint done nothing." Protesting baz sat down with a can of cheap larger and begun chatting.

"Beer, Jay? There's plenty u know"

"You know I don't drink that shit."

"I've told ya, you smoke and I like a lager." He would always justify drinking ten cans of cheap lager in a couple of hours by referring to my pot smoking. "You know he nearly got me caught today, don't ya!" Mel yelled.

"Don't lie. Mel! You rang me up and had me come over here and make a phoney phone call to Ed Rooney." Baz's laughter at his film quote was not appreciated, so before Mel could return the volley I was on it. "Woh, woh I don't need this." Getting up I moved into the kitchen. "What have I said about you hanging around with him?"

"Well I ain't from now on I tell ya he's cut his ties from me." Mel would always say this until the next time. The mood soon mellowed allowing me to relight the roach from earlier and drift in and out of some more daytime telly. The evenings drew in quickly and the house soon filled with friends looking to smoke their pot. Nat, Roy, Tony and Jock were all present. Pipes and bongs had become the in thing at sessions, but nothing came closer to this filthy past time, than the cobra a well crafted evil looking water bong that had gained a reputation for sending even the most hardened smokers, white. Once that lighter was put to the loaded end and you began to pull, finger poised on the chock, bang! It would hit the spot every time.

Tony would always ask Roy who for some reason couldn't skin up to do one for the road and Roy's response was always the same.

"I've gotta get up in the morning."

"So 'ave I, c'mon son." Knowing Roy would give in Tony persisted in a subtle tone.

As the last of the lads left to a barrage of complaints from Mel, I looked at my clock, it read eleven Twenty five, knowing Sam would be round for another instalment of night time TV I thought it time for a cuppa.

So it continued throughout the summer, late nights, followed by the chaos of daytime. My self worth, if I still had any, was lost beneath a pile of confusion. I felt let down, why could I not be like the others? Having the security of a family home with what I saw as supportive parents. To my mother's credit I knew she would never totally abandon me if I needed help, but she had a new Focus in her life. Mondo as we called him and part of me knew she deserved her own space after Twenty five years devoted service to her family. Despite this strange new existence deep inside a part of me knew I would never surrender, a spark of life still told me I was special.

Autumn leaves full of colour made for an impressive view as the last of the summer sun danced upon them. September, a month that always brought on child hood memories was combined with a deep sense of longing. Like the temporary parting of good friends it left me empty for a moment.

Then in one swoop Jock brought me back from my daydreaming. "Have we got to pick Sam up, did ya say Jay?" Watching his hands on the steering wheel I answered him.

"Yep about five thirty mate."

Now golf was never really a game that I would usually entertain, but some of the lads had started going and I suppose the thought of free pot, free golf and a laugh with the group allowed me to escape my miserable existence. Having done the rounds and picked people up Jock drove into the local 'nine hole' and parked up. Strangely enough Scud had decided to join us, strange, because Scud just didn't do sports, but as I thought there is always a first.

Luckily I wasn't the only one who was crap at the sport. Seconds, on a large cone shaped joint was my consolation for hacking my way to the first hole and putting in some ridiculous score. Still I was out of the house that was the main thing. "So you fancy coming over tonight then Dug?" Jock enquired. "Yeah, I have always had an interest in the supernatural, witch craft, that sort of thing." Dugs response was loose. "Well to be quite honest with ya mate I think it's more about life and our part in the universe." Listening in on Dug and Jock's conversation had intrigued me, witchcraft and life matters, what were they on about? Still pulling on the joint I'd acquired from Sam, I broke into the conversation. "Who wants a pull on this?" Jock moved my way.

"Yeah, nice one," came his response. Taking it he walked off. "Hmm" I thought, I was hoping to find out what they were going on about, I didn't like to be left out in the dark about anything and could sense something was going down.

We completed the round and walked back to the car where I quickly enquired what was next. Jock turned from putting his clubs away. "Well I can drop you of if you like, cos me dug, Sam and Scud are going over me mums tonight, she wants to talk to some young people about life." Jock paused a moment. "Come if you like, we'll have some pizza, a few munchies and be back at yours for a smoke before you know it." I found myself hesitant at first, I had never met Jocks mother, only that my own mum had had two run 'ins with her, branding the woman rude. "How long we gonna be over for?" I stressed. "Like I said," Jock confirmed. "A bite to eat and a chat." Not knowing the enormity of that decision or wanting to be left out I decided to go.

Chapter 2

By Chance

As we drew up on Jocks drive, a wave of apprehension came over me, I would have to be polite, remember my manners a whole host of bizarre thoughts ran through my mind. I was stoned, but I comforted myself in the fact that so was everyone else.

Jocks father, a warm looking man invited us in, the house certainly lived up to the wealthy image Jock had always portrayed. So much luxury and detail everywhere things I'd only dreamed of. Following Jock we found ourselves in the kitchen where we were greeted by a small silvery haired woman with a big smile. "Hello boys are you hungry? Help yourselves to pizza."

The food looked great but a sudden loss of appetite came over me, for some reason I felt shy and anxious. It's just the hash I told myself. Knowing I would regret it later once my appetite returned I decided to tuck in. After complimenting Jocks mum on how good the food was, we were lead into a small cosy room seeing an array of cushions and seats scattered before us we spread ourselves out and got comfortable.

Sitting down Jocks mum introduced herself as Jan, then her friend Mindy, a shy looking woman with a fragile frame. Only when the greetings were done did Jan smiled broadly and begin. "You" she began waving a hand in the air and past us all, "are dearly loved and all very special souls with a unique purpose." A wonderful warmth washed over me and her glowing face gave me a sense of security no one had ever told me in such a heart felt way that I was special. "You all came here." Jan continued, "with a very special purpose during this lifetime." Her words resonated somewhere deep inside me and I felt a strange enthusiasm for what she had to say.

"You are most probably very old souls, being here tonight is no coincidence, nothing happens by chance, everything happens for a reason." More positive feelings flowed through me and something unfelt for a long time began to fill me with hope. During the following hour Jan talked about life and how we lived in an age of boundless opportunity to grow as souls. Then something unexpected happened, Jan started talking about how painful events in our lives were opportunities to grow. Looking round she quizzed us for such experiences. Jock was quick to suggest that I had been through a rough patch, turning to me everyone wait to hear what I had to say, a minutes pause and out it all flowed out.

Two years of pent up hurt and frustration, every last drop, my fathers suicide, family, my leaving home, but most of all Emma, the one thing I held dear, 'my inspiration'. Empty and peaceful afterwards I sat for the rest of the evening in silence, something inwardly had changed, but as we left the house one thing that hadn't changed was my addiction to pot and I was gasping for a joint.

"Get one together Sam." I said, in an uplifting manner. Raising his eyebrows he reached for his gear. "Interesting evening wasn't it?"

"Yeah it was good."

"Well, if you're interested, "Jock interrupted "my mum said you can come over every month if you like?"

"Fort-nightly would be better." I pressed.

"I'll ask 'her for ya mate." No one seemed to object and sure enough Jan agreed. The next few weeks were more or less the same, only I had this feeling of hope and anticipation now making it more bearable. The next meeting at Jan's came round quickly. I took what was to be an ongoing seat next to Dug on the small couch ready for what would also become a familiar talk by Jan. Was the experience a fortnight ago real I thought? Part of me somehow knew it was, but I needed the evening to clarify it. Sue and Mindy's words were ever inspiring and did exactly that. Leaving my second meeting I was eager to discover if it had been the same for the lads. Turning to Dug who was skinning up I quizzed him. "What did you think of tonight then?" I needed to know if he and the others felt the same positive charge, giving rise to the new inner feelings that had begun to manifest in me.

"Yeah… interesting… interesting!" Dugs response sounded unsure. "That book Jan gave you looks intriguing, what's it called?" Removing my hand I glanced down and peaked at the front cover. "Way of the Peaceful Warrior." Now, I hadn't read a book since leaving school, but I felt obliged to read it. The book was to become, as Sam referred to as, 'the book of books' and over the weekend I began to read it. Soon hooked I was lead into the world of Socrates and found that reading, made life more bearable putting me by Monday morning in surprisingly high spirits. Hitching a lift to the job-centre with my brother Danny I begrudgingly entered. I never liked visiting the place, it always had a depressing energy about it, but optimistically I browsed the boards.

"Ere you go," said Danny, "eighty pound per week, nine till three, no previous, you could do this." Still standing next to me Danny waved the card around. My heart pounded. Shit he'd found me a job, and one that I could possibly do.

"Well, I suppose." Taking the card from him I read it a second time.

"Give it a ring son." He pushed.

"I will when I get home!" Afraid my response was defensive I hadn't had what I would consider a proper job for well over a year and was terrified of work, or more-to the point thought I wasn't good enough. Returning home I rang the number Dan had given me. It rang a while before it was answered. "Hello," groaned a grumpy voice the other end of the line. Taking a breath I went along with it. "Yeah, I'm ringing about the job for a window cleaner."

"Now, I'm not looking for time-wasters son, but if your genuine come on by me house this afternoon." Taking down the address I rang Sam to borrow his car. Sam was good like that, he never said no to me borrowing it, and came over.

"Aren't you gonna put a shirt on?" He enquired. Tucking my T shirt into my jeans I looked up. "I got a funny feeling it ain't that sort of interview Sam; anyway get one together will ya."

"Already have." Relighting half a joint he must have smoked on the way over he pulled hard.

I don't know, you full time junkies, I wouldn't want to fuel your habit." Sam would always joke about the fact he was only a part time junkie because he worked. Taking the joint from him I smirked. "Well, I'll be like you soon, won't I?"

"Oh good does this mean your gonna buy some pot?" Throwing me his car keys he wished me luck and laughed.

Chapter 3

The Window Cleaner

I arrived at the house hoping deep down inside I was going to meet my own Socrates like the one in the book. I knocked to the sound of a small dog barking.

"Go and lay down, Penny." I heard bellow from behind the door. Weighing up the grey haggard figure in front of me I simply stared a mo before speaking. "I've come about the job, I spoke to you earlier."

"Come on in son, i'm Mack, Mack Cartel."

Going through I scanned the paintings and photos hanging along the hall wall, entering the kitchen I sat at the table. "Cup of tea," Mack croaked. Looking round at the state of the kitchen it didn't appeal much, but I accepted out of politeness. For the next two hours I drank tea from a dirty mug while Mac sipped super brew from a small glass and told me his life story, at the end of it all he had begun repeating himself over and over. "So you defiantly want the job then son?"

"Well, yeah!" I said feeling drained.

"Good…good and you say you can drive?"

"Yeah I've got a licence." Realising the time, and the need to return Sam's car, I had to get going but just couldn't seem to find an opening to get away, Mack just wanted to talk and talk. Assuring Mac I wouldn't let him down I began backing out of the house. As I put my foot down hard on the accelerator I felt good about my new job to start. Mack seemed genuine enough and it meant I could finally sign off the dole.

Another late Sunday session left me feeling shit Monday morning, hearing Mel up I got her to drop me off for my first morning at work. Opening the door Mac appeared worse than I remembered, only this time he wore a black woolly hat covering the grey and making him look like a convict. Ushering me in Mack begun preparing our equipment. "You see Jay." He said holding up an ice cream tub with a worn belt attached to it. "I'm a thinker do you know how much they want for one of these mop, pouches in the shop? Twenty five quid! Hah…twenty five quid! But you know me son, I'm a thinker, 'ere you are, does just as good a job." Taking it I waited for what was to become a ritual cup of tea each morning before leaving the house. As we drove to the first house Mack set about explaining the ins and outs of the job, also of the many innovative tools he'd personal crafted to get the job done. The morning was slow, but peaceful and I began to reflect on a few things Jan had said to us at the previous meeting.

"The material world is an illusion, all this around you isn't real and thoughts are things, you're so lucky to be here on the planet at this time." How could this world be an illusion? It was real, and if it wasn't how could I look beyond this illusion? If my thoughts could create, why couldn't things happen as I wanted them to? I was a big believer in the power of the mind; my father had often talked about moving objects with it, along with believing that an all powerful force existed like in the film star wars. The day soon ended, Mack paid me what I'd earned and it felt good with the exception of Wednesday when it rained, leaving me and Mack little else to do other than smoke and talk the week passed quickly. Whilst Mack drank more special brew from his small whisky glass, I simply sat and listened.

By the time my next meeting with Jan came round I was on a high, I'd found a job and I was reading my book. Going in we got comfy and waited for her to start.

"Well, Jason's got a job with his own Socrates." I frowned at Jan's remark, if only, I sighed. Eventually she spoke about a group she'd attended and a Mr Leason who ran it. She explained how he was a much evolved soul, and had a firm understanding of the esoteric teachings, that they would learn from him. After hearing her out, I sat and pondered. What did it mean to be evolved? And how did one know, if he was indeed, evolved? Jan had already made reference about us all probably being old souls, so perhaps I too was evolved.

It was toward the end of the meeting that we all met Jock's brother. Jimmy had long hair and dressed very hippy, or new age like, he had a wonderfully calm manor that was complimented by the peace he carried. Like my own, Dugs first impression was that he looked like Jesus. After listening and talking to Jimmy I felt perhaps he was my first example of an evolved person, he seemed to have a firm understanding of life and what Jan had been telling us about. In the car on the way home our usual conversation continued. "He's sound, Jock's brother." Dug said as he pulled out his skins.

"Yeah nice bloke," I agreed. "Did you understand what him, and Mindy were talking about toward the end?"

"Some, bit mad though weren't it mate." Sealing the joint Dug shook his head and smiled. Pulling out of Pots village Sam spoke for the first time. "Going back to your house then Jay?" In all the excitement I was experiencing from the meetings it was becoming obvious that others didn't find things as interesting, the unrest in Jock was now apparent by the way he'd left the meeting, Scud was struggling to stay awake, while Dugs logical mind seemed to be struggling to grasp some of the info, as I discovered at the Friday night session in my house it didn't stop there either. We were all early into it when one of those incredible Baz stories occurred.

"Your brothers off his trolley Jay, I tell ya." Roy suddenly blurted out.

"What's he done now?" Resigned to the fact it couldn't be good I waited for it.

"Last Saturday, I had last orders and decided to walk back with Moss and Linx. We came down over the iron bridge when we heard all this beeping looking round we see this shuttle bus pulling over. I thought it strange because it was well late for a bus service. Anyway, it pulled up alongside us and the doors swung open, looking in I didn't recognise him at first, he was all suited up shirt glasses and everything, smart really."

"Nah," I found myself saying.

"Yeah, it was him, at first I thought he had a new job, but it turns out he'd nicked it from the bus compound for a laugh."

"So what did you do?"

"Well we was half cut anyway, so we got on, he said he'd drop us off, I tell ya, it was outrageous the way he pulled away, I lost my footing fell back and found meeself on the floor...When he hand braked outside Linxies house well we just all pissed ourselves laughing mate." Daring to speak I sighed. "What did he do with the bus after?"

"He said he had other people to pick up before dropping it back to the compound, ees crazy Jay."

"You don't need to tell me mate, I dunno how he gets away with it." As one subject closed the next quickly opened.

Having spotted the book by my side Tony had picked it up and was now holding it in the air. "So what's this all about then?"

"It's really interesting it's all about life Ton…well sort of."

"Who'd you get this off, Jocks old dear at one of those weird meetings that you go to?"

"They're alright Tony… I just find 'em interesting that's all."

"Na it aint for me mate, I don't know how you sit there all night."

"He wants to be Jesus." Bill interrupted bringing a laugh from the crowd in the room. I began to sense I was leaving myself open to cheap jokes. "So what do you do then at these meetings?" Tony continued.

"Just talk about life mate." I glanced to Dug and Sam, for support but quickly noticed Sam's reluctance to get involved. Quiet, he just kept rolling his joint.

"Do you dress in holy robes and prance about?" Bringing about more laughter Bill looked pleased with himself. "Shut it Bill, what the fuck do you know about anything?"

"Ooh… Don't get all heated mate or well begin to think you do!"

The ribbing was becoming a bit unbearable but I was torn between my friends and what I was learning at Jan's. This is all I needed I thought, given it was usually me giving out the stick. I wanted my friends so much to feel what I was feeling and for this reason it made it hard to accept the stick. "Shut up you idiots!" Usually Mel's moaning would put a bad buzz on the evening, but it came as a welcome break from the stick I was taking and helped divert it elsewhere.

The weekend soon passed and I was back at work Monday with Mack. We were over the other side of town working when Mack asked one of his, off the cuff questions. "Sorry, did you say you played football, son?"

"Yeah, love it Mack."

"Never been my cup of tea son, prefer to kick back in front of the box with a beer meeself."

Football had meant a lot so far in my life. It was something that kept me going through those dark and depressing moment's it gave me something to live for, nothing really came between me and my football. Tony had once remarked. "If you could eat and sleep with footballs Jay, you would."

And so the day flowed with similar questioning. During the following weeks it became obvious that Mack was struggling with work, his relationship with alcohol was bigger than I'd imagined. Seeing things were going to fall apart I got a small bank loan out which I bought a cheap car with. Leaving Mack at home to sort himself out I was soon going it alone. The big advantage of being alone was it gave me plenty of time to think, Mac still took sixty per cent of the round which I dropped off every night over a cup tea and a couple of royals. With festivities on the way I wanted our first Christmas in the house together to be special. Mel sorted some fab food that I cooked while Dan did what he did best, provide weed to smoke and make a good fire.

It was over dinner that Dan piped up, stoned and drunk his humour was anything but savoury. "So when you gonna take that round off the old man then?"

"You would think like that!"

"He's old and weak. Just fill him up with whisky one night and it's all yours." Stoned Mel broke into uncontrollable laughter choking on cherry aid it spurt from both nostrils. I too found myself laughing at his sick humour, but something inside told me taking the round of Mack wasn't the way forward.

Chapter 4

Indian God

It was in New Year that the meetings dwindled down to just Sam, Dug and I; it was also at this time that Jan began to introduce new things to our meetings. The introduction of meditation brought quite a stir of emotions, not just in me, but everyone else. The biggest introduction was the awareness of Sai Baba a subject Jimmy loved. "He's a cosmic avatar." Jimmy remarked over our ritual cup of tea that would take place toward the end of each meeting. "He is not of our planetary system. He's just visiting." Jimmy then produced a photograph. For a moment first impressions made my mind run riot. "Who the hell is this guy? I thought. He could be the devil in disguise, the false prophet my old man kept harping on about when I was a kid. "What, and 'he's god?" I eventually remarked. Smiling as though his life depended on it Jimmy sat back, "defiantly."

"Like the hair do." Sam said sarcastically.

My gut reaction was caution, but there was a strange feeling that surrounded the character on the photograph. Looking at Dug I could see his logical mind thinking, pondering and digesting his internal thoughts. Dug's peculiar unconvinced pale expression made me laugh. If I was struggling with it what must he be thinking? People's reactions made me smile. Before leaving Jan felt it important that we should find our point of evolution. Seeing our confused faces she begun to explain.

"Your point of evolution is a measurement of your soul's journey towards becoming a higher being all I require is your signatures." Reaching for the table she picked up a pad and passed it over to Sam who was closest. "I'll take them with me so that Mr Leason can analyse the energy surrounding them, he will then determined how far you have all come." It sounded like a good idea my ego could do with a boost and I felt sure that I'd be the most evolved person in the meeting as the pad came round I wrote it down and smiled.

. Leaving that that night the need for a joint was stronger than ever. "Load's to take in tonight." I said to the others who were silent. "Well, get one together then Dug." Amazingly, Dug could skin up anywhere and in record time without a single crease, his skinning up knew no boundaries, from a moving car to the summit of mount Lomond in driving rain, he could roll. A far cry from the saggy nappies Sam would all so often roll. As the smoke hit my lungs a sense of peace followed and I relaxed into my thoughts. How evolved was I? I could be a stones throw from being a master. Master Jedi Down, I had to be up there somewhere, I was different special, I'd always felt it. "You gonna smoke all that?" Interrupting my thoughts Sam nudged me...

The next day was a come down, rain and work, it's amazing the way people looked at me cleaning windows in the rain, by ten thirty I'd had enough. A news paper a packet of Virginia and a quiet spot to contemplate. Sitting in the country car park I could feel the all too familiar depressing thoughts once again sweeping over me, the roll up failed to help, and the Man united cup exit displayed across the second page just deepened the feeling. "This is bollox!" I said aloud, I just can't take it anymore, why me, lord... a real deep feeling of hurt, loss and anxiety was now pounding me. Taking my own life despite contemplating it was not an option. The example my father had set was not acceptable. Chicken shit way out, I thought. I despised the feeling, where was my luck my big break, I'd always imagined myself having. Mentally torturing myself and feeling sick in my tummy I drove home as recklessly as my hundred pound motor would carry me. Curling up on the sofa, the anger and despair gave way to sleep. Apart from the shit of that day the following fortnight went by quickly with little incident accept for the farcical display of ignorance by Baz. It was on one of his unexpected visits that he turned up bored all I asked him to do was go round the pet shop and see if there were any kittens for sale, nothing more. Two hours later he returned with a black Labrador called Reg and wonders why he stretches me in every way…

Wanting to take more in myself and Dug got into the habit of not getting stoned before we went to Jan's. As we approached Pots village I quizzed him. "So what do you reckon about this point of evolution thing.

"I'm not sure I fully grasp what she means, or that I'm convinced."

I turned to face Sam. "What do you think?"

"Umm yeah dunno really." Realising neither of them had anything to say I gave up. After the usual introductory talk by Jan, she passed back our signatures. What I read was hard to swallow. "So explain it again, Jan." I asked. "Well there's, five stages of human evolution to becoming a master. There's the physical, emotional, mental and spiritual. The other, is your personality, isn't it Mindy?" Jan looked at Mindy for reassurance. "Yes, your personality, Jan that's right." This meant I hadn't even passed the first level and what made it worse, Sam was more evolved than me, how the fuck could that be right, point eight the same as Dug. I could sense Sam's satisfaction at the results, he didn't gloat, but he didn't have to, I could just feel it. It was a massive hammer to my ego, more failure I thought, I'd gone from Jedi master to boot boy. "I wouldn't worry too much, the great Elvis Presley was only a point nine and look what he achieved." Mindy interrupted. For the rest of the night nothing sank in, in fact it was all a bit of a blur.

All the years of thinking I was a born leader and now nothing. Upon leaving the urge for a splith was massive.

I woke heavy and lethargic I didn't really fancy work and hoped that it was raining. I poked around the ashtray for a decent sized roach or enough butts to make a one skinner. Sitting back I begun to roll and drift into my thoughts. I am special and different to everyone else, I'd always felt it since I was little so how could I be point eight, I mean no way was Sam more evolved than me. If it wasn't for me, he wouldn't even have any friends. That's not fair I heard my conscience say. Until recently, I'd been in control of everything. It was me that made things happen and me who inspired people to do things that previously they thought they couldn't. It was I who brought the possy together, oh, all I needed was a break, but it just hadn't come. I presumed my life would just come to me, that things would just fall into place. Why had things become so shit, I quickly lit the one skinner I'd now assembled. All the quizzing and dwelling was just bringing me down.

Within a few weeks March arrived I had always enjoyed spring somehow it refreshed my senses. I didn't like working alone and needed help with the widow cleaning round. I hoped that my decision to take on the tangled ball of string Baz would help us find new ground as brothers. I didn't tell Mack, who quickly became known as the "Mackalander," a crud nickname from one of the many films Baz would quote from. I still respected Mack, but needed to see how my brother would perform before allowing him near this frail man.

At first things went well. "Listen I've been thinking Baz, maybe you can drum up some business for us on your side of the city, you know make a start to building up our own round."

"No problem, Todd I'll get right on it." He quoted. Sure enough he rustled up some new work that very weekend. Give credit where it's due he could talk and convince people of anything, given example. We were collecting round money one night, when a customer asked me what else I could do work wise. Before I knew it, the tangled ball of string began to flow. "Yeah mate, what you interested in?" Oh my god, I'm thinking.

"Well, can you do building work?"

"No problem." Baz continued. "What you got in mind?"

"Well a bit of garden work, maybe a barby... that sort of thing." Baz had seen the green light and was now off. At first I was quite impressed by his suggestions and enthusiasm, then walking down the side gate it happened.

"We'll put a wall here, the barby there, trellis up the back, fast growing vines, a bit of ivy, Micsomotosus... that sort of thing." Well if you just missed it like the customer, I didn't, and shrank seriously back into my shell. And so it went on.

March and April flew by, bringing with it the end of a dreadful football season. Back in November I'd been voted out as manager with Dug replacing me. They said it was because he didn't play but it caused friction because in my personal opinion, Dug just had no passion for football what so ever. In -fact the team would have folded if Dug had his way, however an emergency meeting in a hotel conference room combined with an eighth of solid paid for by the in trouble club funds, and the vote was passed for me to finish the season.

Sitting there I thought of all the important business meetings that must have taken place in this quaint room, and yet here we were skinning up, drinking beer and passing our own important decisions, for me it was a great moment.

The season ended well with a notable win over my Brother Danny's team. Notable because he had made our lives hell all season, his rude jibes and cruel comments on how crap we all were had just kept coming. Not to mention the fact that he was personally going to punish us all individually, come the big day.

The match itself was one of the best ever played there was a great energy surrounding it and just about everyone in town was there to watch it. We found ourselves with a slender and stable lead throughout the whole game, then with ten minutes remaining Dan broke free. One on one with the keeper, and knowing how fantastic he was at football I knew his moment had come. But it was a strange irony that day. Filling, in for us with his one and only ever appearance Baz the tangled ball of string was our goal keeper. With the goal at Danny's mercy, Baz saved superbly in front of the all the lads and onlookers. What an end to a season and my first example of true karma…

Chapter 5

Something Magical

It was just before the end of season football 'do' that something magical occurred. On hearing the phone ring I contemplated answering it.

"Is that Jay?" Came, a pastel tone I instantly recognised.

"Alright Jimmy," I said somewhat surprised, "You what."

"Yeah, we need another driver for the Croatia trip can you help out for a week?"

"When do you leave?"

"Tomorrow morning." My initial reaction was Jesus. "Can I ring you back in twenty minutes while I think about it?"

"Course you can." With that he was gone. Putting the phone down, I instantly ruled it out. I've got work I thought. Football; things to do I told myself in a vain effort to hide my fear, nah, not me what can I do. Jimmy had told us all about his recent trip to Croatia taking aid to the refugees was something he enjoyed. He was a man doing things. Then it clicked, what an opportunity. Where's the great adventurer, you can do it, Jesus, yes I can do it. I immediately picked the phone. "I'm in Jimmy, what do I need?"

"Basic stuff, you know."

By that night I'd gathered together some loose belongings. Dan's sleeping bag, a load of tinned and packet foods along with a change of clothes. Once done I rung my mother. "Don't worry mum, I'll be fine." And so the conversation rolled. "You just look after yourself, d'ya, here me." I hadn't seen or spoken to her recently but her concern was over whelming.

"I know mum, look I'll see you in a week. Love you." Putting the phone down, I buzzed with excitement and apprehension. "I still can't believe you're going." Dug commented from the front room he liked to lounge in.

"Tell me about it. C'mon pass that joint it'll be another week before I have a puff."

"You told everyone yet?"

"Na not yet, I suppose they'll find out at the footy presentation tomorrow night when im not there."

"Can't believe your gonna miss it ya little fucker. What did you tell Mack?" Dugs words were a mixture of laugh and smoke.

"Nothing I'm leaving Baz in charge, Mack won't know I'm gone, providing Baz don't screw up." Pausing I inhaled. "I think he'll be alright for once." Knowing Baz would want to impress me I figured giving him the responsibility would be a good thing. Before leaving that night, Dug gave me a hug and shook my hand. "Good on yer mate, I'll see y' in a week."

Restless and unable to sleep I tossed and turned. My mind was racing I wouldn't know anyone and they were bound to all have experience I didn't.

31

What would they make of me? They were bound to be do gooders. "Jesus, get some sleep." I told myself. Waking on time I readied my things to the sound of Mel filling and boiling the kettle.

"How long you got? She called up.

"About five minutes." Still feeling anxious I charged downstairs and joined her for a cup of tea. Lighting a fag I slowly sipped at it. "Look after yourself wont ya; you know the worlds screwed up."

"I will, don't worry." A knock at the door left no time for long goodbyes. Picking up my things I felt an overwhelming feeling of love towards her, I'll be back I thought, feeling humble I stepped outside.

Jimmies girlfriend Vicky greeted me. She was a lovely girl a bit of hippy about her, but sexy with it. "Jimmie's opening the back if you want to put your things in it." Moving round the back I was surprised to see just how much aid was crammed into the transit. "Hello." Jimmie said. "You ready?"

"Ready as i'll ever be."

"Then let's, go meet the others at the service station." With his usual smile Jimmy got behind the wheel and head off. He told me there were about a hundred and eight vehicles on his first trip, but as we pulled into the services I was surprised to see that the convoy was considerably smaller, no more than about nine trucks. While Jimmy greeted and talked to everyone I was once again gripped with nerves and anxiety, so I decided to stay in the transit. As I sat there feeling all-awkward a tap on the window took me by surprise, looking round a shaven haired lad about Jimmy's age stood grinning at me. Winding down the window, down I waited while he spoke. "Alright mate. I'm Chris, good of you to join us on such short notice."

First impressions I liked the guy, something told me we would get on. Still anxious I stuttered somewhat. "No worries glad to help..."

"Got any puff?"

"Nah, only fags," I pointed to the packet of B&H on the dash.

"Good job I've got plenty then." To my surprise he flashed a large lump of hash before me. "Catch ya later then." With that he was gone. Jesus I thought. Realising it was the same Chris, Jimmie had mentioned from his previous trip, he was nothing like I imagined. Jimmy and Vicky soon returned and we were finally off. The ferry crossing was smooth and by the end of the day we were somewhere in Germany. Talks between the three of us were brief, eventually we pulled into a German service station for the night, knowing I'd finally have to meet the rest of the crew my stomach churned a few times. I watched Jimmy leave the vehicle I couldn't hear what he was saying to the others only that he returned very quickly. "We're going to stay here tonight." He gestured at the grass verge in the car park. Getting out I headed to the back of the van and retrieved my pack. On my return I saw a few of the other volunteers had started putting up tents, going over to them I sat on my sleeping bag and lit a fag. Turning from his tent a well dressed guy smiled. "Hi, I'm Jonathan. Fancy a beer?"

"Yeah that will be nice." Taking the open bottle of beer from him I sipped at it.

"Is this your first trip?"

"Yes, have you been before?"

"Yes." His smile was broad and warm. For the next few minutes we sat in silence, a relaxed comfortable silence then it was broken. "Hello, lad's." Turning I saw Chris pulling on a large joint, opening another bottle Jonathon passed it to Chris. It was obvious they knew one another by the instant conversation that broke out. Behind them I noticed Jimmy was erecting his second pop up tent, seeing this helped me break into the conversation. "Where you guys pitching your tents tonight?"

"Tent," Chris sounded surprised. "Nah, I'll sleep out 'ere in the open tonight."

"Sound's good." I heard myself saying while trying to stay cool.

"Jonathan." Chris gestured with the spliff.

"Yeah cool." He replied on taking it.

"Get one together if you like Jay." Knowing my skinning up skills were pretty poor I was again surprised to hear myself saying, "yeah, no problem." Catching the bag of tobacco and gear Chris threw me I set about putting some papers together. A few minutes later a few of the others came over to join us. Conscious I was skinning up and that not everyone might approve I immediately felt awkward.

"This is Miky." Chris said introducing one of them to me. "He's our photographer Jay."

Rising I shook his out stretched hand.

"If you don't mind Jay," he said, "can you use rolling tobacco in that joint, I ain't to keen on ciggies." Chris nodded to his tobacco pouch. Strangely enough it turned out to be a bit of a touch as rolling backy was easy to skin up with and the end result was quite pleasing. Feeling more comfortable amongst my new comrades I lit up. "I must admit." I said you guys are nothing like I'd imagined."

"What were you expecting?" Miky asked over their laughter.

"I dunno, a group of Sunday school teachers or something maybe." Despite their laughter I was suddenly conscious again of the fact that one of them might just be a Sunday school teacher. With everyone now present I surveyed the group while puffing. The whole thing had the feel of a sixties commune, but they were all very different, big Ken and his mate Miky, a crazy lad named Paul, Jet and Sonia the mystics, Roger the team leader and a handful of others who made us up to about twenty warriors.

As the evening grew cold it encouraged people to retire to their tents and sleeping quarters. Suddenly sleeping in the open air lost its appeal, so I went back to the van and settled down across the front seats. Laying there I looked up at a picture Jimmy had stuck to the dash and pondered over the little man in his orange robe and afro hair. At first my feelings were positive toward the picture of Sai

Baba, but the dark thoughts my father had fuelled me with arose and slowly crept in, what if he was the false prophet…

I woke around five thirty and despite my uncomfortable sleep, I felt pretty good. Looking out the window I saw the mist had shrouded everything; the feeling reminded me of quiet and still night's I'd spent on the river banks. Night's I'd fished from dusk till dawn, a place of cherished peace and freedom confirmed by the early bird singing out its morning song. Knowing I was next in line to drive I should have just got my head down for a further hour, Instead I found myself unable to give up the morning outside and just carried on enjoying it.

It had been dark the night before leaving little to see, once some of the others got up and begun milling around I took the opportunity to take in some of my surroundings.

Making my way over to where we had all been sitting the night before I breathed and absorbed all before me. "Wow!" Rolling hills coupled with picturesque villages swooped across the land and around the odd lake. "Beautiful in it?" still in a haze I hadn't noticed Chris approach, sitting cross legged on the ground he begun making himself a roll up.

"Fantastic!" Stepping back slightly I sat down next to him. Taking the pouch he passed me I set about making my own smoke. "Jimmy thinks we might have to stay here a while this morning, there's something up with the lorry." Chris made reference with his finger to the seven and half ton Ken had been driving.

"Any idea what..."

"Dunno, but they'll find out." We finished our smokes in silence before turning to join the gathering group behind us. Jimmy briefed us on the Lorries break down informing us that we might have a while to wait and to keep ourselves busy. Busy, I thought moving away how can anyone busy themselves in a car park? Just then my attention was drawn to Miky who was juggling, something I couldn't do. Moving closer I watched before speaking. "Any tricks?"

"Some." Smiling he proceeded to show me a few of the simple ones he knew. Glancing through the moving balls for a split second he caught my eye. "Fancy a go?"

"I can't juggle."

"It's easy." He raised one ball. "Here you are, try."

"I got no chance." But as the balls were thrown toward me I knew protesting would be a waste of time. Miky pulled another two from his pocket and proceeded to throw one after the other up. "Just see if you can pick up the rhythm of two balls...Like this." I watched him before spending the next hour dropping the balls in my pursuit to juggle. Miky said if I grasped two, three would be easy, well I'd grasped two and still had no idea on three. I was about ready to quit when it just clicked. Somewhere in my head it made sense then thought turned into action. To my delight, I could do it. Rotating the balls three times I smiled with satisfaction.

As morning turned to day it became apparent that the truck problem was more serious than they thought. While waiting juggling turned to football, then back to juggling then finally the smoking of a roll up. In some ways it was a blessing because I got to know everyone pretty well, especially Chris. I couldn't put my finger on why I was drawn to him maybe it was his wild attitude, or the fact that people seemed to accept him for what he was, something a part of me seemed to struggle with. Still harbouring a bruised ego I sought out new ways to please people for their approval. The need to be liked was as strong as ever. Feeling weary from a long day in the services we were back on the road Jimmy looked very tired remembering part of my purpose was to drive on the trip I brought it up. "You want me to drive, Jimmy?"

"Tomorrow," came his patient reply. I turned to Vicky who was shuffling a deck of cards next to me. "Fancy a game?"

"Okay." She said with her lovely broad smile. "Let's try this. See how many cards you can guess when I hold them up." Guessing only about two cards from the complete deck the game wasn't as much fun as I thought. "You're supposed to telepathically tell the person whose holding the cards." Jimmy chuckled.

"How...?"

"Just send it out, as a thought form of energy."

"Like a Jedi mind trick?"

"Something similar, yeah."

"Fancy another go Vicky?"

"Sure. Go for it." I began to think, how do I send this? Until slowly I began to submerge myself completely into the eight of hearts, trying to show Vicky through my eyes and just for a moment I felt a strange connection to her or something. It happened so quickly I almost passed it off. "Eight of hearts."

"No way." I said turning the card.

Smiling Jimmy kept his eyes on the road.

"Try again." Vicky said, but it was not to be repeated throughout the rest of the game, but that tiny moment stayed with me. Jimmy drove for about an hour past darkness before pulling over for another break at a large service station. We found a parking space at the far end with picnic tables that served as a good place to set up for the night. Once sorted, I sat and waited for the crew to mingle.

"Beer, Jason?"

"Yeah, nice." Jonathan was the first to join me. A sense of mellowness came over me, yeah, this was alive I thought. Miky and the others quickly joined us for beers whilst Chris worked on large tobacco joint. It was becoming a real feeling of comrardry with the purpose of our journey and what may lay ahead clearly put to one side. In a sense this was good, as I felt it helped to maintain a positive feeling in the camp.

The x-army feather bag I'd borrowed from Danny proved to be a real plus in the night. It was early hours when a bus full of Germans woke us all up.

Spying half a roll up amongst the empty bottles of beer was my call to move. Behind the wheel at last, the European motorways proved to be a real plus point; the convoy speed wasn't fast making for easy driving especially when your passengers are asleep.

Our journey through Austria was stunning. I'd never seen more beautiful settings they were unique and would stay with me always. The turquoise reservoirs enchanting villages and snow capped mountains filled me with surges of inspirational energy. Long tunnels bore through whole mountains before descending into timeless valleys, leaving an impression on my subconscious that would eventually surface in the mountains of north Wales. Yes the great explorer in me was alive and kicking.

Austria's experience served me well for the long journey through Slovenia into Croatia. A large lay by made a good stopping point just outside Zagreb. The first of many games of football gave some light relief while we waited for our guide into the city.

We didn't have to wait long, behind the wheel for the final leg of our journey into Zagreb Jimmy took over the driving. My first impressions were not as I'd expected. The city was full of movement and had a very Western European feel to it. While people went about their daily life's restaurants were thriving, and bars were full of people. Jimmy told me that our contact lived in the same street as the Croat priminister; it wasn't long before we were heading out of the city and into quiet plush looking streets. Pulling onto a large driveway, we finally reached our first destination. A radiant looking woman greeted us warmly and led us into a large house. A big room had been turned into a dormitory that would sleep about ten, with two smaller rooms for couples and women; finding a spot I bed down my sleeping bag. I was unpacking a few clothes when Jimmy appeared in the doorway.

"Anyone hungry, Gita the house keeper has prepared some food for us."

"Great and lovely." Were some of the comments that greeted him.

Chapter 6

T with Baba

Tired and hungry I followed the rest of the crew down the hall and in to a large dinning room, upon entering I was greeted by warm smiles and shown to a seat. The table was laid with a variety of good food and drink. Acknowledging the spread with a warm smile I glanced about the room, the walls were covered in giant framed pictures of Sai Baba that held my gaze. Bringing my attention back to the table, I began to tuck in with everyone else. Feeling my every move was being watched, my eyes were drawn back to the pictures all around me. Baba's eyes had a Mona Lisa quality following my actions it made for an uncomfortable meal. Filtering out the dinning room Jimmy made a beeline for me.

"What do you think of the pictures?"

"Great."

"Come with me. Let me show you the meditation room."

Following him we made our way to the end of another hallway. It was an exquisite very beautiful room, like a temple only decorated with Indian artefact, silks and paintings of Baba. Despite sitting and attempting to meditate, I just wasn't perceptive to the energies and soon found myself giving Jimmy a weak excuse to leave. Being late I made my way back to the sleeping quarters and settled down.

I pondered why the pictures made me feel uneasy and why the need for proof just wouldn't go away. It didn't matter how many times Jimmy told me of all the good things this being Baba was doing, I still needed to feel it and see it for myself.

Chapter 7

The Game

Waking early in an apprehensive haze, the thought of visiting Rekeichi our first refugee camp turned my stomach and gave me anxiety. Up until this crucial point it had all been a bit of a laugh, but now I was going to be faced with the realities of war.

I don't remember a lot about breakfast or our journey across town only that Jimmy's mood was chirpy and talkative where-as I stayed quiet, and totally focused on being useful. Wondering what my roll might be and what would be expected of me, I pondered all the way. Reaching the edge of town, we pulled into the refugee camp and parked beside some of the wooden makeshift houses, as we did so a large crowd of women and children begun to quickly form.

"So what d'ya want me to do then Jimmy?" I enquired.

"Just be yourself." His comment wasn't exactly constructive, I'd of preferred to be given a job. Climbing out the transit onto the dusty floor, I looked over at Ken who was already handing out boxes of aid. Jimmy was busy opening the back of our truck before doing the same. Joining him, I held up my arms.

Vicky passed me a box. "Go and find someone who needs it." I hated being put in such awkward situations. Sighting an old woman outside one of the wooden houses I went over and offered her the box, she was more than happy to accept the gift so I returned back for another. And so it went on, handing out boxes in the blazing heat to those whose need was greatest. Strange really because I didn't have a clue what was in them, I just assumed they contained the essentials. Deciding it was time for a break, I went over to see what Chris was up to.

"You ok Jay. D'ya, want a drink?" Seeing Chris boosted my confidence. "Yeah nice one, I just feel a bit lost mate." It was in this moment someone threw a football to me from the back of the van. "'Ere you are Jay have a break, have a kick about with the lads over there." Seeing Ken with a whole bag of footballs instantly lifted my spirits, it was something I loved and I felt excited. "I'll have a kick about with ya Jay." Pointing to the crowd of kids congregating Chris motioned to them with the football suggesting a kick about. One of the older kids could speak English and helped sort out some sides on a dusty old piece of land. For the next forty five minutes or so my heart danced and laughed at the way these kids could kick a ball about. Knowing we were due to return to the camp later that evening me and Chris arranged another game before going back to box duty.

Arriving back at Rekeichi later that evening the place had a real buzz about it, back from odd jobs or work they had found in town there were a lot more men about the place. The young lad who could speak English was full of smiles and greeted me and Chris. He was quick to lead us away from the crowd back to the dusty pitch we had played on earlier, to our surprise they'd managed to erect some make shift goal posts, standing beside them looking at us eagerly were a dozen expectant footballers. Going back Chris gathered together the rest of the male volunteers to make up a side. A growing crowd I presumed were family and friends had started to gather around the right hand side. The sides were seven of us v twelve, thirteen maybe fifteen kids all varying in age I guess, and so we kicked off perhaps the best game of football I have ever played. The skills on show from the young lads was superbly impressive, we sweat we smiled we laughed.

Winning and competing merely dissolved into a free flowing exchange of energy between the two teams. As dusk loomed practically the whole camp was present, the score was five all maybe, next goal wins, who cared, but it was all adding to the ever increasing high of the evening. As we peppered their goal with shots, one of their lads picked up the ball, skipped pass two tired players and delicately lifted the ball over the advancing keeper, fantastic. Seeing the people embrace the evening as though it was a carnival lifted my spirit I felt part of a larger community and comfortably humble...

Arriving back at our digs everyone fancied a drink out on the veranda. "What I want know." Chris said. "Is why those people thought you played for Man United Jay?"

"Because, of my short's." I laughed. "They just didn't seem to grasp that I only supported Man United before I knew it they had me signing footballs, scraps of paper, shaking my hand, hugging and everything. I Guess I just went along with it." Everyone was now cracking up at my comments. "How come when you hugged those girls they called you Johnson?" Miky added in amusement.

"They hugged me." I said bringing about more laughter. "As for Johnson they just didn't understand that it wasn't my name." Drinking with high spirits carried on till late, only then did people begin drifting off to their beds. Gesturing to the end of the garden Chris smiled at me. "Fancy ducking out for a spliff?"

"Yeah sounds good." Sneaking of, we found a quiet spot sitting down I waited while Chris got to work on one of his tobacco cones.

"I'm glad you came on this trip." At first I was a bit taken by Chris's comment, it stirred warm emotions and my approval issue I had recently become aware of.

"Yeah, it's good it's opened my eyes mate." Watching Chris as he lit the cone, I saw a very beautiful soul. He had a wonderfully light honest charisma that lifted me when I was in his presence. "So what do you make of this Baba character?" his unexpected question jolted me back. "I don't know really, I am open I think, I can't say it doesn't confuse me at times." I took the joint before continuing. "I do struggle with this word, 'Devotee' and the need to have his picture everywhere."

"Yeah, I can relate to that. These trips have certainly opened my heart people I've discovered genuinely want peace along with sharing."

I soon became aware how uncomfortable I was with this relatively deep conversation. I use the term deep as it wasn't so much what Chris was saying, but the manor and depth of his voice, he sounded like a man ready to open up. Not ready for this I quickly changed the subject. Laying in bed later that night it bothered me how affected I was by another man's intimacy, yet at the same time I was quite honoured that a guy I'd only just met was ready to open up to me, like a trusted friend.

Chapter 8

Forgotten Orphanage

During morning breakfast Jimmy informed us that Gita had suggested we take some of the aid to a large children's orphanage about an hours drive away. Happy to do so everyone agreed. Heading out we soon left the outskirts of the busy city and begun making for the baron country side. Aware that we hadn't passed a street or house for miles I wondered what lay ahead. As the hour approached we drew up to a large derelict manor house in the middle of nowhere.

Driving through the rusting gates we pulled up on a large un-kept drive. Getting out Jimmy wound the window down. "You guys wait here, I'm just gonna go and knock." I watched Jimmy make his way to the large doors, looking over his shoulder he stopped and knocked. He was soon greeted by a women in what looked like a nurses outfit, returning to the truck he called for everyone to form a group. "It seems it's a place for handicapped and mentally ill children, they're quite happy to receive as much aid as we can give them, according to the nurse it doesn't get offered often, but it might be a good idea to go in and look around first."

My heart raced, I was more anxious and nervous about this than any refugee camp, it wasn't that I didn't have feelings for these people, more a case of whether or not I could deal with the situation...

Sensing this Vicky smiled and reached out, feeling her squeeze my hand I decided to stay near to her. Inside a grand staircase now in decline was before us, as people headed off in different directions I followed Vicky and a few others upstairs where a nurse greeted us. Smiling she led us down the corridor and into a room. Entering it, my heart just broke. Children with bodily or facial disfigurements, every disability I could imagine and some I couldn't were before me. Some were even tied up which I learned later was for their own good. Within thirty seconds a feeling of worthlessness came over me and I stepped out of the room. Following me out Vicky stopped me.

"Are you okay?"

"Sure, sure."

"C'mon lets go in the next room." Apprehensive, I followed her into a dingy little room with failing light. Inside it were baby's loads of them just laying inside cots, going a few feet before me Vicky stopped. "Here," she said lifting one of their small palms. "Just hold their hands and give them some love." Kneeling down beside one of the cots I realized I didn't know how, I mean what could I do? Feeling distressed I left the room and headed straight for the exit.

The hot sun hit my face, sighing heavily I made my way over to a mound of dry earth and sat down under a thirsty looking tree. Tears began to roll down my cheeks, pull yourself together I told myself, a few deep breaths later I just sat observing the line of ants working hard in front of me.

"Marvellous aren't they?" It was Jonathan. "A perfect social family they are." Jonathon helped bring my disillusioned mind back to earth. Feeling conscious I'd let the side down I spat it out. "Sorry I felt a bit lost in there." "Don't be hard on yourself, you aren't the only one, I don't think you'll ever see things like that again, mate." Jonathon's comments were welcome and lifting feeling more confident I got up. Heading back to the entrance we saw that some of the others were moving the stacked aid into the large hall. I hadn't really chatted to Tommy before but as I took a box of aid from him he spoke. "How can god allow these things, what does this Baba fellow Jimmy follows say about this then?" His obvious emotional state made my own voice at first a touch gentle. "Well I've been told it's like this mate." And out came my answer. "James believes in reincarnation and karma, how you choose to pay back that karma, is up to you. One way is your reincarnation with perhaps physical or social dysfunction, this helps with personal growth and rebalancing, does that kind of make sense?" Tommy, stared at me a moment as if weighing me up.

"My sister is physically handicapped you saying she was a bad person in her last life?"

"No, no not at all, it could be a mixture of lifetimes. Some people see this route as a good way to clear any unwanted karma, not as a punishment, but to

51

aid they're own growth and those around them, so as bad as it looks it can be a positive thing for all those involved." Where did that come from I thought, I'd read about it and heard James talk about it, but never quite expressed it myself in such a fluid, positive manor.

Anyway it seemed to work Tommy's response was light and thoughtful. "I guess I can relate to that." Arms full of aid he went ahead.

Going back to Gitas was a quiet affair in comparison to the previous high. Aware we would be leaving for home in the morning I found myself in a very reflective mood. I'd experienced something new, felt the explorer deep inside and touched a moment's bliss. My life seemed to be moving, a part of me now begun to understand certain feelings I'd had since I was young. There was a bigger picture and I had a roll to play.

The journey back to England had its usual twists and turns, but eventually after two days we were back home in Buckingham, realising the adventure was over didn't dent my high, the camaraderie and companionship I'd built up amongst the team had given me a purpose. Walking through the front door I dropped a quick hello with my stuff and went straight out to see who was about.

Usually heading out alone came with a paranoia buzz, probably brought about by dope but not tonight, I felt as light as a feather and full of life nothing could have knocked me.

Chapter 9

To Much

The following meeting at Jan's, I was highly charged and full of excitement. One of her long but interesting stories helped to calm me down but still I couldn't wait to relay my experiences of the Croatia trip to the group. A chance to talk came towards the end of the evening when Jan and Mindy went to make the ritual tea, a bit of chit chat and laughter and stories broke out. As the conversation slowly moved away from Croatia, Mindy introduced us to another interesting character Maîtreya.

"Who's Maitreya?" I enquired.

"He's the Christ," Mindy said, "the new world teacher."

"So he's Jesus Christ?" Dug asked.

"Not exactly, he overshadowed Jesus during the last three years of his life he is the embodiment of the Christ principle." What she was saying went straight over my head. I got the feeling Sam and Dug were just as bemused as me by the look on their faces. Just back from work Jimmy joined us and was instantly pressed by Dug. "Do you know who this Maitreya character is, Jimmy?"

"Sure, would you like to see a picture of him?" Without further word Jimmy dug out a post card, handing it to me I saw a bearded man in white standing amongst a crowd of Africans. Taking it from me a sarcastic smile crept across Sam's face. "Yes but who is he?"

"He's god," Jimmy proclaimed "the new world teacher."

Frustrated I quizzed Jan. "Hang on. You told me Baba was god, so who's this guy?"

"No." She quickly added. "I told you, Baba was a cosmic avatar. It's all in the wisdom teachings by Alice Bailey we learnt it at Mr Leasons."

"How did you hear about Maitreya?" Dug pressed.

"Well." Jan continued. "Benjamin Crème gives a lecture in London on the reappearance of the new world teacher."

"There's a lecture in a fortnight." Jimmy interrupted. And so the mind blowing conversation continued until we left.

As we drove away that night my mind was wandering all over the place, my Croatia high had been replaced by a feeling of frustration and the little voice in my head was telling me it had all become a bit 'too much.' Back at work I counted out the days takings while Mack made the tea. "Hey Mack, can I have one of your royals?" Mack smoked the royals due to the fact that they contained five extra cigarettes than that of a normal pack. "'Help yourself son." As I lit up he went off on one.

"Do you know why I boil my water son?" Smoking the royal I shook my head. "Well let me tell ya, do you know how much it costs to run an electric kettle, hah double maybe triple!"

"Great." Strange really I was quiet and shy around Mack. I'd always hoped to find some wisdom in the things he told me, like Socrates' from the book, but all I saw was a broken man, beaten down by the system. Almost immediately a strange thought came over me, but did the system really beat Mack, I mean he was forever coming up with ways to get one over on it no matter how small, from kettles to cable TV, car boots, social, the list was longer than I imagined. "I'm getting a new dog on Thursday son." Mac smiled while carefully pouring his pan of hot water over a cup.

"Oh yeah wot sort?"

"An old English sheep dog named Max." I didn't bother to ask any more, instead my mind returned to the conversation I'd had at the last meeting. Leaving Mack's I pondered on my decision to go with Jimmy to Ben Crèmes lecture in London. I couldn't help thinking it might be good Jimmy said that Maitreya would over shadow everyone and that the energies would be potent. I'd heard about people having blissful moments in the presence of these higher beings or in the process of meditation. I'd enjoyed some interesting experiences myself, but others always seemed so much more. Things were never quite as sensational for me as I'd been told. Take drugs for instance I just never seemed to reach the same level as the guy next to me, they always seemed to be on another planet while I stayed on earth, who knows maybe I would experience a blissful moment if I went. No sooner had I thought this than the old fear rose, 'the false prophet', your being sucked in. "Christ!" I called out, give me a break, my inner dialog could be very confusing at times.

The following weeks passed quickly and before I knew it I was on my way to London with Jimmy, Dug and Vicky. Arriving in Euston we parked and walked to a large lecture building called the 'Friends house.' Entering the building myself and Dug made anxious conversation. Leading the way upstairs Jimmy carried his usual relaxed and knowing energy with him. After heading down endless corridors, we all made our way into a packed lecture room and took our seats. Scanning the room I saw that microphones had been placed on a large desk I didn't have to wait long before a white haired man calmly walked to the front of the room. Pulling a chair out he sat down only when the room had calmed to a quiet atmosphere did he begin.

I listened intently as Mr Crème offered positive solutions to world affairs and the coming of a new world teacher. Over the two hours he spoke, many of his solutions made simplistic sense, until finally we came to the blessing part Jimmy had spoken about.

Doing my best to stay calm and detached from my expectations a real sense of anticipation came over me. The lights dimmed and I gathered we'd started by the way the people around me had closed their eyes. Having been taught, to breathe by Jan I practised it, as I did so good and bad thoughts flowed through my mind and the room temperature seemed to increase unless of course it was just me. Either way my mood was becoming irritable, then a sense of calm would ensue. The whole thing was beginning to become a bit of a let down so I opened my eyes. Looking at Mr Crème I saw him very calmly observe each individual until his eyes caught mine, feeling self conscious I quickly closed them again. Now I just wanted it to finish, but it seemed to go on longer than the fortnight leading up to the event. Finally with a sense of enlightenment it all ended and people moved about the room again.

Seeing that Dug was quite impressed with the whole affair I kept my wandering thoughts to myself and made my way with the others to where the car was parked. As we walked down one of the streets a man on the corner of one handed me a leaflet, it read, 'the anti-Christ.' That's all I need I thought discarding it quickly.

The journey home was a lot more refreshing and made for good conversation. Talking to Jimmy helped me put a few things into place. "So, Baba is an aspect of god the same as Maitreya only Baba's from another system while Maitreya evolved through ours?" Searching Jimmy I watched to see what he had to say.

"You got it." He smiled. Remembering a planet Jimmy had previously mentioned where masters resided in peace. I pressed him for more answers.

"Tell me more of where the evolved masters live, and more of Sirius."

"What do you need to know?"

"Well how do you know when you're a master?" Inquisitive Dugs eyes also searched Jimmy for some answers. Jimmy went on to explain about the five stages of evolution Mr Crème had previously mentioned. "When you express total control over your personality, physical, emotional, mental and spiritual vehicles, you are free of the reincarnate cycle. Then like the Buddha, you can go and live on the planet Sirius, or like the master Jesus, stay and serve this planets evolution."

"Nice." Dug confirmed through a broad smile. "I think I'll go straight to Sirius myself."

Come the next meeting, Jan had a new exercise for us to try. 'AUM' she said "is the cosmic sound of the universe and when sounded will help centre you, especially when sounded twenty one times which we will be doing tonight." 'This is going to be embarrassing were my initial thoughts, it's all gone a bit far and if Bill could see me now he really would think I'd gone off my rocker and have a right laugh. "Let's have a practice." Jan said. "If you sound the 'AAA' and let it flow into the 'u' and finish on the 'm', you'll be close to the sound we're looking for."

After the initial practise we closed our eyes and sounded the 'Aum' twenty one times. It wasn't so bad, a bit like singing in a group, good or bad our voices blended together. While Jan went to make tea for our break Jimmy came in and joined us. It was over the cup of tea that I discovered he was a vegetarian and entered into another new conversation with him. "So why give up meat?" I enquired.

"It might taste great." He went on. "But there's no energy in dead flesh."

"What you talking about, it's full of goodness."

"It may serve all your physical needs, but it has effects on your emotional and mental vehicles, as well as being very grounding. "Can't see how that works?"

Jimmy patiently went on to explain his theory on energy. "Everything vibrates at a certain level. Your whole being is made up of vibrating atoms and these can be affected by negative and positive thoughts. A lot of the meat you eat has come from slaughter houses where the energy is very dense and the animal welfare has only been secondary, so when you consume this meat, you consume this energy."

His comments meant little to me. I couldn't see myself giving up meat, not in this life time so I dropped the issue. The journey home was a mixture of emotions. Sitting quietly I assessed the past six months, there had been so much information and so much promise yet inwardly it seemed little had changed. My world was still up and down yet I had to acknowledge a braver side of me. The Croatia trip and getting a job, perhaps I was looking for miracles. My thoughts started to drift and I begun pondering over Emma. A year had now passed and despite a string of girlfriends no one seemed to match her. Growing up together, she was the girl next door with similar interests to that of my own, we just seemed so right; she was the only girl I seemed to be myself with.

Despite the pain having eased over the passing year, I'd somehow allowed my heart to become closed. Somewhere in me was a spark of light shrouded in darkness and I knew I had to find it again. The summer ended quickly and September arrived. Sipping morning tea I casually allowed my mind to wander, I could feel the joy I'd experienced in Croatia and the good, Jan's meetings had installed into me and my life. Yet that familiar September melancholy feeling stirred in my belly and gave way to change, deciding to go back to college I knew my time with Mack had all but come to an end. I was also moving back home away from the mad house that had been the beginning of my awakenings, with my sister away living with a friend and Denis having bought his own house, there seemed little reason to stay.

As for the tangled ball of string, he too was embarking on his own journey a whirlwind romance, had lead him to marry. I'd hoped this may be a chance for him to calm down and make something of his many talents, but only time would tell.

Also winding down were Jan's meetings an overdose of information had caused Jock, Scud and Sam to drift away. Dug still went, but my feelings were that he was back on one of his long obsessive stints. More importantly within myself, I knew it was time. I had enough knowledge to chew on for now.

I decided a letter was the best way of telling Jan that I was no longer able to attend. One can always say what he wants in a letter without being interrupted. Armoured in my new found knowledge, the coming years would be good. I was gonna fly. Putting my thoughts aside, I stepped out of my car...... it was my first day of college.

Chapter 10

New Beginnings

A couple of golden years had promised so much but as autumn ninety six rolled in, college was over and my application for uni, rejected. With no permanent work it had left me a little down. As Dug left the flat to go home the familiar September feeling washed over me. I could feel a sense of worthlessness returning; not now, surely I'd come through so much and I'd learnt so much, yet here I was alone in my flat stoned and slightly lost. My string of failed relationships had got me to thinking about Emma once more, after all these years there she was still in the back of my mind.

The phone brought me back to earth allowing it to ring a few more times, I lazily answered it. "Jay I need you downstairs." I didn't think to ask why; the thought of avoiding anymore feelings and thoughts was enough to venture down into the ground floor flat where my brother Dan dwelled. The place was really just a big terraced house converted into two flats that Dan had bought two summers ago. Reaching his door I pushed it open. "What do you want?" I asked in a pain staking tone. A large belch followed by his crude stoned laughter told me it was nothing serious. "Get us a Stella from the fridge, Jay."

"You fat faggot, is that what you called me down for!"

"Come on, you know I'd go, it's just me elbows playing up." Why he made reference to this old football injury was beyond me. "Anyway," he continued. "There's a good programme on about aliens thought you might wanna watch it." The thought of green, tea and TV would get me past thinking for another night so I resigned myself to getting him the beer.

October brought with it the dark nights, these only added to my gloom. Part time labouring for Dan wasn't helping, it seemed life had hardened him up over the years and I soon became the brunt of his moods. He would often tell me, compared to others how little I'd done with my life. Caring little for my meditation and universal ideas, he'd often challenge me, but not before quoting how well he had done what with owning the flats. "I mean where's, the universe got you your nothing without money." He would often make this reference on the journey to work. Knowing how sceptical he was I muster up some vocal energy. "It's not always about money, Dan."

"Well." He snorted with contempt. "The universe ain't got you very far has it boy? You need to stop dreaming." His co worker and football buddy Rick would nod in agreement while I sat in the back of their filthy run down work wagon. "Your, just lucky I'm here to keep you boy." This Dan enjoyed.

Don't bite, don't bite I would tell myself, but part of me was beginning to think where had all this universal thinking got me, and of all the people, why him, why had he done well?

Another long weekend passed, Sunday evening I could just hear Dugs vehicle as it sped away back to London where he now lived and *worked. With no work of my own lined up for the week ahead it was becoming obvious I could* no longer hide from my depressive feelings, my inner battle was raging, part of me refused to acknowledge that I could become depressed again, whilst another part seemed ready to accept it.

Had I just papered over the cracks hiding out at college, and had I really moved on.

'Feel the fear and do it anyway,' Jan had once said, but do what exactly?

As I began to face up to another helpless week, a feeling of not wanting Monday to come, and not wanting to wake up thrashed through my soul. Realising nearly four years had passed since my first meeting at Jan's and feeling that I was back to square one, was the final blow. I'd finally landed at the bottom my low was fuelled by thoughts and feelings. Uni rejections, job rejections, relationship's perhaps Danny was right, where had my faith in the universe got me, nowhere.

Wallowing in my worthless state tears fell more freely and my heart pounded out a tune of sadness, very gently I told myself I like Jason and I don't want him to die, a sense of uneasy emptiness followed. Embedded in the moment my entire being had become one with my mood.

All was still when a voice replied. Tomorrow hasn't come yet. The script is still unwritten so make it a good one. On hearing these words my whole energy changed. They became more than just words, my heart laughed out loud and my mood turned to joy because in that moment my whole being seemed to resonate with something larger and a bigger realisation dawned, for all my exterior failings that seemed to want to break me inwardly my spirit could never be broken. As I lay in bed I set about imagining the most amazing future starting with Monday.

Waking early was a mixture of anticipation coupled with nerves, what first? How can I make things different? Leaving the bed I strolled to the kitchen, a morning meditation I thought, yeah meditate it was something I hadn't done for a long while, in fact when was the last time, taking a glass of water I moved into the lounge. Getting myself comfortable I took a deep breath and began to let go of my usual mind activity. Focusing on my breathing I placed my total awareness on the inhale and exhale. I began to relax and slowly let go, I continued with my breathing until all was still and a sense of calm was about me. I asked my soul to help me to connect once more. I envisioned brilliant white light filling my being I imagined myself merging with my higher consciousness until I began to feel a full sense of connectedness to the higher current. It was a space I'd forgotten about, I asked my higher self for advice and help on my current situation, the response was profound.

You've been waiting for someone to save you, a magic wand, call it what you like, but its not going to happen, hearing these words from my higher self unnerved me, then this cold reality rolled over me. I had to do it, the only person that had the power was me, the realization came with an anxious fear but before this fear could settle my higher self spoke the words. 'Feel the fear and do it anyway.'

I suddenly grasped the affirmation from the little book Jan had given me on a chance meeting that summer and my energies lifted once more.

Upon finishing my meditation a third realization struck me. Knowing knowledge and realising knowledge were two different things.

Feeling more determined than ever I wrote out a list of changes, the first being to stop smoking pot.

Feeling my first test in the downstairs flat that evening I watched Dan skin up. Of course he found my new plans amusing and sniggered "You've failed so why bother." I swallowed Dan's banter and condemning comments and went to bed that evening hash free.

I could no longer allow myself to be held back by fear, my list stared me in the face there was no going back, applying for a job at the local rail depot was a success and within a fortnight I'd started the job, changed my diet to a much healthier standard and still not smoked.

. My whole mood had slowly transformed, meditation was maintained leaving a sense of balance about me. Finally, the last thing on my list was an art exhibition. Upon failing entry to university, I'd vowed to the tutors at college that I would not give up and would prove it by putting on an exhibition when enough pictures had been painted. At the time, it was nothing more than a boastful response to my rejection I was now going to make it happen.

Setting out my paints and placing my canvas onto the easel I was full of energy. Slowly as I stared at the blank canvas I began to doubt, the longer I stared the more my energy waned. Just at the point when I was about to put off starting, that wonderful affirmation from that little book flowed through my thoughts, 'feel the fear.'

Chapter 11

The Works

The first day of my new job was a little flat. The rail depot, or the works, as it was better known was a series of huge run down workshops built about a hundred years ago. Covering an area the size of a village, this once this proud place had employed ten thousand people and could build a train from top to bottom. Falling into decay and ruin most of it was no longer used leaving nothing but a ghostly feel around the workshops. The only plus point was I knew a few of the workers including my good friend Bill. Up until now, me, and Bill's friendship had been largely built on free flowing banter, and knick-names, but this was different, I was now entering his work domain. Taking me to one side his tune changed completely and I saw there was another side to Bill.

"People respect me 'ere, call me by my first name and know nothing of my life outside this place, so if you don't mind, keep the banter and nicknames to yourself. I really wished Bill hadn't said that.

The works was full of colourful characters making it easy to settle in and make new friends. On the home front I had done my first painting and was preparing a second one. Taking some of the old bed sheets I stretched them over wooden frames, but still I needed a main theme, something I was familiar with. Then it came to me, my friends would provide it, best part of my life had been spent with them getting stoned at sessions, the coming trip to Amsterdam over the New Year period would not only make a great theme but give me the chance to make good use of my camera too.

Since changing my diet which now included raw vegetables, water and green teas, a real sense of purpose had come over me, and life felt good.

Cancelling my trips to the fried food van, I begun cooking instead, the creativity I found in the kitchen whilst making meals for me and Dan was like an extension of my art work. Every area of my life begun to flow I'd even found some voluntary work teaching the kid's art, at the local scout hut where my mother worked. For the first time since Croatia I was being of service.

Amsterdam came quickly, the chaotic new-year celebrations were loud but my mind felt very balanced while watching them I begun to contemplate the year I'd had. My thoughts turned to Lisa, a girl I'd met at college. Although the relationship hadn't worked due to my ego pulling the wool over my eyes, I recognised how her love had helped me to love again melting the ice I'd placed around my heart after Emma had left me. I'd learnt to love again and I would always be truly thankful to her for that. I'd come through the big high and down to the bottom of my pit only to rise up and truly start living, pushing through my fears and breaking old habits, I was ready for nineteen ninety seven.

The new- year brought with it a creative flow that produced canvas after canvas of colourful paintings. I was determined to keep going even if it meant giving up favourite past times, things that brother Dan found hard like watching the big game on sky and getting stoned, truth be known I think a part of him had found it hard, me taking back the energy I'd found in my life.

The city church had an excellent viewing gallery with plenty of natural light, for this reason I hired it for the weekend to display my own works. The opening date was in May near my birthday.

February however brought with it a shifting mood. Without being aware, I began to slack on my meditation and it wasn't long before my old personality started to amuse itself at work. I'd slowly surrounded myself once again with the in crowd and, the new people brought back the old approval issues.

They were all good lads, but enjoyed a good doss, rude jokes written about one another on the toilette walls grew into a mass of graffiti and insults especially about Bill who also seemed to have been drawn away from his Conservative hole. Given the fact he worked with an obsessive queer called Tim, and another called Doggie the potato I was surprised it had taken him so long.

"Give us a lug of your fag, Max." (Max was Bills real name)

"But you don't smoke Tim." Bill replied.

"I know but it would give me the chance to taste your lips." how he had the cheek to tell me people respected him I don't know, if these were the kind of characters he meant. The toilettes seemed to serve as a place people could air their rants about colleagues and managers. Some had a poetic feel to them, others just plain crude, more and more I felt myself slowly going back into my ego, showing off and allowing my rebellious side to take hold. For as long as there was a crowd, I played it. The euphoria that I had felt so true was wearing off, the less I meditated the more unbalanced I became. Old eating habits slowly crept in, trips to the burger van in the mornings with the lads, and cups of coffee. Then by the end of February the first cigarette crept in, despite theses lapses I still felt good but my new way of life was quickly de-railing. It only took, but one big bust up with my brother Dan and the first joint passed my lips.

Mid way into March the creative streak that had seen my most productive art period was slowing. Going half's on a new car with my brother lifted my spirits, so I splashed out on a few other things I could afford but the buzz was short lived and the need for something else once again grew.

A chance conversation with Dug brought up the subject of hiking and so the adventure rose up in me once more. This was the antidote I needed for my restlessness. A couple of other lads were up for it and so a place and date was set. We would head for Snowdonia national park in the mountains. None of us were really prepared for the grand beauty of Snowdonia or those rugged mountains, my spirit soured amongst the changing colours of the landscapes, the wind and the elements, it was just the camaraderie amongst friends I loved. The feeling of freedom and moment to moment awareness was like living a meditation upon the mountain. It was time cherished and a trip never to be forgotten.

Coming back from the trip was hard, sitting down with a cup of tea I broke into a flurry of tears, the trip had brought up a feeling of aliveness in me and made me realise how my new way of living had slowly failed, it was as though those few months, everything that had flowed had been no more than a crutch to get me back on my feet. Remembering I had a job and an art exhibition to look forward to I tried not to be too hard on myself, I was becoming more aware that it was what was on the inside that really mattered not the outer.

I worked hard during the month of April and come May I left the flat for the new city church with my art- work.

There was a lot more to hanging pictures than I'd anticipated, so I was grateful to Bill who had offered to help me. Putting the final piece in place we both walked around the circular viewing dome until we were back at the entrance where a small table littered with handouts on my work was. Sitting down I looked up at the large banner we'd hung. It read "a celebration of life." Taking in a deep breath a surreal feeling came over me,

I'd actually done it, done something for myself, an immense feeling of happiness welled up in me, a feeling, almost too good to be true.

Closing my eyes I thought of my father, from an early age he had been my artistic inspiration, I'd watched him produce canvass after canvass of meaningful pictures. I knew he was proud and dedicated my first exhibition to him.

"There's a little cafe out front, fancy a cup of tea?" Bringing me back from my high Bill awaited a reply. "Why not," I said. "I've earned it."

"Milk, Sugar?" The woman asked as we waited. That was when another realisation dawned. "Just milk thanks." I replied. Then it hit me, despite all my other habitual failings sugarless tea had stuck. Jan's voice brushed through my head, small gentle steps, she was right and best of all the penny had dropped.

The art exhibition wasn't to be the start of a long distinguished career, but it turned into a personal triumph that proved I was capable. June rolled in, and with the art exhibition behind me a sense of boredom prevailed. I had become a paradox to myself and those around me, who perhaps didn't understand my inner journey for a deeper meaning to life. Some even began to view me as a hypocrite, and in lots of ways they were right, I did still allow my personality and ego to run riot, whilst claiming I had begun to understand my spirituality.

Painting one night in my art room my lack of conviction frustrated me. Glancing round the room I spied the aging photo of Sai Baba that

Jimmy had given me all those years ago. A part of my heart had wanted to believe that the afro Indian could be a master or god, but another part had never been able to. Pondering the Indian a sense of anger welled up. "What makes you so special?" I blurted aloud. "How come you're a god?" Not expecting an answer I looked in the opposite direction where I noticed a pile of newly acquired books, the top one read quotes, by Sai Baba. Picking it up I opened it randomly and there was my answer. It read. 'I am god, so are you god, the only difference is I am aware of it, you are not yet aware of it'. Smiling at the statement I sat down. This meant only one thing. I would have to go to India myself.

For the next few days I toyed with the idea before deciding to confide in Dug, sitting in the car out it came, well sort of. "Ere Dug, fancy going to India? Visit the ashram for ourselves."

Given the years we'd spent sharing spiritual experiences and discussing practically every aspect of spirituality along with Sai Baba. I felt confident he would say yes. "You little fucker" He shrieked. "When did you hatch this idea?" smiling at me the signs looked good, so I told him about my experience and the book quote.

"So you're really serious then?"

"To right, its time Dug we can do it." I pressed him.

"Yeah I'm in." Dugs agreement was my first real step to going as I wasn't prepared to go alone. Needing solid information on how to get there and back I thought of Jimmy who I knew was living in London.

Driving down to Camden with Dug the familiar euphoric mood that came with new dreams and making them happen could be felt. Dug was pleased with the ease in which he navigated his way through London however Jimmy's basement flat wasn't so easy to find. Eventually parked across the road from it we venture towards it and knocked.

It was good to see Jimmy again. "Hi guys." He smiled. "I thought we'd go for a walk through the park." Relaxed as always Jimmy lead the way. Bearing of from the park we walked along the canal. It was peaceful talking pleasantries in the sunshine. A small cafe serving camomile tea allowed us to sit down and discuss what we had really come for. "So, what d'ya guys wanna know?"

"Everything," I said." You know, hotels, money, visas!"

"Okay, okay, but when you going first?"

"We thought November the twentieth." Sitting back I smiled.

"Yes good time to go weather wise, you'll also be there for the birthday celebrations."

"Really," Dug looked surprisingly pleased.

"Yeah, so it'll be busier than usual, they reckon over a million people pass that week alone." Unsure how I felt about this comment I continued to listen. He went on to explain that we had to be over twenty five or we needed a guardian to sign us into the ashram. Driving back my decision to go was finalised cemented in my mind, I was defiantly going.

It didn't take me long to tell everyone what we were planning, the excitement was all too much. The prospect of seeing, believing and following my new goal renewed my purpose and excitement about life, but then it came, the big downer after a smoke in the car. Having changed his mind Dug tried to be tactful.

"Why?" There was an edge of astonishment about my voice.

"It's just isn't my time mate and I'm worried about the heat, you know I burn easy." I pressed my case hard. "That won't be a problem Dug, come on, you got to come. I can't understand why you wouldn't, after all these years we've talked about the universe. C'mon, this is it our big chance to go and live it." Dug silently shook his head, the thought of India alone I just didn't fancy but his body language told me he'd made his mind up. "Sorry mate I've thought about it and I don't want to go." Nat who'd been skinning up in the back piped up. "You still gonna go Jay?" A flush of dizziness came over me and my fears began to show, then boldly I committed. "Course i'm gonna go."

"Good on ya, you'll be alright." That night as a few lads came over and asked me about the trip it felt good to be bold and reinforced my commitment to going.

Waking early, a sudden rush of anxiety came over me, I'd never even been outside the UK by myself, let alone India, how could I have let my ego get me into this. A cup of tea and a dirty roll up served as a mild distraction. "Universe I need help, guide me please". I'd now got use to the idea of asking out loud as an answer usually came to me even if it did take a few days but not today, today was to be different. Pondering my dilemma I moved into the lounge. There on the sideboard was a pile of unread books, two by an author I hadn't heard of, picking them up I read the back of the first. It was about following one's path and finding one's destiny so I started to read it. By lunchtime I'd finished it. That small novel the Alchemist had swept away any last minute doubts, I was going.

Dropping into the bank after work, I decided to apply for a loan. The money would serve for both the trip and doing up the flat. Within half hour I'd got it and three thousand pounds had been deposited into my account.

Heading to London served two purposes, first my ticket, next my visa.

Then came the real anxiety, I'd never considered pot to be a problem before. During the day I was excited, come night, I was stoned and terrified. I could no longer hide from the fact that it brought on bouts of paranoia and anxiety especially about my trip. Pot only seemed to serve my overactive thoughts about what I might find in India, but there was no going back now. My time leading up to the trip was up and down. Finally after a meal with close friends in Camden I found myself in a black cab heading back to Dugs flat with him and Jock. Dugs flat was based a mile from Heathrow making my morning departure easier to deal with. Up early Dug drove me to the airport. Still wishing that he was coming I stood shakily in the entrance of Heathrow airport.

"You'll be fine." Smiling at Dugs comment a humble feeling came over me, picking up my rucksack I walked positively into the airport. Doing things yourself as I discovered brought out inner strengths twinned with sharp decisions. Navigating through what appeared to be a nightmare airport became a positive exercise that flowed smoothly. My luggage was checked in leaving me to chill in the departure lounge, reaching in my back pack, I pulled out the Baba book and new diary I'd brought for my trip, both came in handy to pass time before boarding. Once on the plane, I found my seat and the engines roared. As the plane pushed hard down the runway I felt a huge surge of emotion, my family, my friends everything that had become precious to me rose up in a wave of sentiment, then a strange hollow feeling followed. I don't recall much of the eight hour journey to Bombay accept for the enormous amount of fear I generated through having no one to lean on.

The queuing and flashing of passports brought some relief from my negative mind activity, still feeling a little shaken by the whole ordeal I sat down in the departure lounge. Purposely pulling out the Baba book I held it slightly higher than normal and begun reading it. I was just getting engrossed when a London speaking Indian addressed me." Are you heading to the ashram?" I lowered the book.

"Yeah...Well I had plans to stay in Bangalore."

"Best head straight for the ashram." Turning the Indian pointed. "The American couple over there are going to share a cab and the fair, would you care to join us?" I immediately felt drawn to the idea, so I told him I would consider it during our connecting flight. Tagging along with someone who knew the ropes would be a useful blessing, but I felt bad about breaking my own reservations. This thought continued to plague me during our connecting flight, what would be best.

Touching down in Bangalore my mind was made up but as we filtered from the plane, I couldn't see the Indian guy and my anxiety returned. Moving on to collect my luggage I caught sight of him, but he appeared to be leaving and my luggage was late. Shit, I thought just as I'd made up my mind. Looking around for the American couple, they too were not to be seen. A calm voice within my head told me to let it go what will be will be.

Closing my eyes I drew breath through my nostrils till my lungs were full, holding it in for a few seconds I then positively released it alongside all my doubts, panic and anxieties. My energies lifted and I told myself, I am Jason, the great explorer, who fears nothing, within the space of a few seconds I had become a giant. Spying my luggage I threw it confidently over on my shoulder, head held high I marched towards the exit. Reaching it I felt ready to face India.

Outside my Indian man from earlier approached me. "Are you ready to go to the ashram?" smiling I gestured he lead the way.

Chapter 12

The German, Fasting and Baba

Lack of sleep made the taxi ride feel like something out of a dream...Wearily I listened as the American couple filled me in on Baba stories, but I only caught bits because of the way the guy drove. As though he had a death wish the taxi driver got faster and faster. On a mad mission he over took the cars in front again and again sometimes losing the dusty road altogether for a few seconds. "Jesus, do they all drive like this?"

"Most of them do." My Indian friend replied. "Anyway where do you think you'll stay in Putterparti?"

"One of the hotels if we ever get there."

"You're not going stay in the Ashram? The village is full of chaos and Baba advises against it." The Americans comments brought about a shot of anxiety; I went on to explain that I would stay in the ashram, but was under twenty five, hence needing a guardian. "If its Baba's will there'll be room, you don't go see him, he invites you." For the next ten minutes, I pushed the issue of needing a guardian until the Indian gentlemen offered to act on my behalf. Despite having already made reservations in the village, it felt right and my new friend guided me into the ashram, and through the check in procedures. Once inside we puffed a sigh of relief and looked forward to relaxing. "Come." The Indian said. "I'll take you to your sleeping quarters."

As we walked through a large complex of flats and overloaded dormitories it hadn't occurred to me there would be other Western people until we finally arrived at the last dorm. Upon entering it was pretty packed with tents and nets, trying to avoid them I followed my guide towards the end of the dorm. Seeing a couple of guys packing what they had tightly together the Indian stopped. "Are you guys leaving?"

"Sure." One of them said. "You want the nets and mattresses?" My Indian man looked at me with a smile. "You see Jason, Swami has already taken care of things."

I allowed the journey and the amount of fear I'd generated over the whole idea to flow through my mind, I then smiled in amazement about how easy it had all been.

My first venture into the village was to change up money and buy some appropriate clothing. On my return to the dorm a tall blonde guy about my age addressed me.

"My name is Zonk would you care to come with me to Darsham?"

Caught out by his comment I blundered a bit. "What now?"

"Yes, its afternoon Darsham, shall we go?" With no time to think I found myself following Zonk out of the dorm. We walked a while before I broke the silence. "What is Darsham?"

"Darsham is a very wonderful experience the swami walks amongst us leaving hearts full of incredible love." Although I'd heard about this amongst other things from Jimmy I still didn't allow my expectation level to rise. Small talk about where we were both from helped me along the way until finally we arrived at the entrance of the Madera. "Now we must wait." Pointing to the large queues growing before us Zonk gestured for me to pick a line in which we would wait. Choosing one we sat and waited in the sun. Jesus, I thought, how long do they expect people to sit and wait in such clammy condition's nudging me, Zonk spoke and my answer was almost immediate. "This is good, we are line number three."

"What does that mean?"

"That we sit at the front very close to swami." The word swami was a new to me, but it seemed to be the chosen word people referred to as Baba. Zonk was right about the line, we had chosen and It wasn't long before we were shepherd along and into the Mandera. Once inside the building the immensity and detail of the structure became very clear, shuffling along we searched for somewhere suitable to sit. Stopping Zonk smiled. "This is a good place Swami will walk right past us." The floor was cold and hard but I was happy to be out of the heat. This is it I thought I was finally going to meet the being who claimed to be god.

As thousands more people slowly filtered in I patiently waited, and just as slowly despite my best efforts, the hard floor soon became uncomfortable. In an effort to stay calm and lift my energies I decided to meditate, at first with a therapeutic effect but my discomfort soon caught me up again. Jesus, hurry up I thought.

Patience another voice expressed and so for around ten minutes a bout of mind activity twinned with physical discomfort toyed with me. I was pushed to the point where I just wanted to leave until finally like a kettle switching off at boiling point, a strange sense of calm came over me. Closing my eyes and taking a deep breath, I re -opened them. My ears tweaked to the sound of soft Indian music, draw to the far end of the Mandera I saw that it was at last the Swami.

As I caught my first glimpse of the little man dressed in a full length yellow garment a renewed sense of excitement came over me. Gliding effortlessly amongst the women at the far end the Swami stopped to talk and receive their letters. It wasn't long before my mind activity kicked in again what would I say to him? Would I get a personal greeting, or interview. No expectations, I repeatedly remind myself. My hopes got the better of me until the Swami begun moving gracefully toward me. Had my moment arrived was he going to stop and speak. My heart began to pound like never before, could this be it the truth, could I really be in the presence of a master? Finally he came within touching distance and a strange thing happened. I couldn't look up from his feet,

I felt frozen it was like I was waiting for him to summon me, touch my head, talk I don't know, anything to get my attention. Closing my eyes for a few seconds I breathed deeply and waited, but nothing happened. Opening my eyes, I quickly saw my moment had passed and that the Swami had moved on. Having experienced nothing my emotions raced, No feel of bliss, acknowledgment or the deep sense of love that Zonk had expressed, just a huge sense of deflation now surrounded me. Then came a voice in my head, remember no expectation you said. Tired and hungry I made my way back to the dorm, realising I'd been on the go for over thirty hours with little food or sleep, I slumped down onto my mattress and drift effortlessly into a cosy daze. Dreams flowed to the point I couldn't be sure what reality I was in, all the anxiety and stress was replaced by a feeling of safety and warmth and it felt good.

. The sound of shuffling and moving woke me, checking my watch, it was three twenty AM. I'd been asleep nearly twelve hours, next a raging thirst came over me I needed water. Half a litre later and my eyes began to adjust to the dark. I was now aware someone was performing what looked like Thai chi, slow deliberate movements that looked very therapeutic shadowed areas of the room. Incredibly, despite no previous experience, I felt drawn to stand and begin to move in a similar fashion. Stretching and breathing the whole experience soon brought on a tranquil state. As people began to wake I was brought back from my comfortable state, called it a day and headed for the showers. The cold water despite the morning heat took my breath away and left me feeling invigorated and alert.

Back to my mattress I wondered what time things would get going, I didn't have to wait long to find out. Despite still being dark, there was no mistaking the familiar German voice of Zonk. "Jason I see you are ready?"

"Yeah but it's still way too early I think?"

"No this is good, Darsham queuing starts at five am." Jesus I thought, you mean I've got to rise every morning at this hour. Appearing at the entrance of his tent he glanced toward me. Making our way to the Mandera that morning I felt as light as a feather and carried a real positive vibe with me. Zonk explained how he'd felt immense love coupled with a blissful feeling during the previous Darsham, from my perspective it sounded great. Entering Zonk was surprise that we ended up sitting in the similar spots we had the previous day. Looking around and toward the front of the Mandera I noticed other Westerners with cushions, back rests and other sources of comfort, as the hard floor pushed into my ankles a sense of envy came over me.

The long wait was uncomfortable but I managed to contain similar mind activity to that of the previous day. Then the music kicked in and the Swami appeared. I tried to keep a balanced energy about myself, but once again my expectation levels rose. I wanted a personal interview it was the only way to be sure. As Baba drew closer my heart began to race again. I wanted the bliss

Zonk had experienced, I wanted the knowing that Jimmy had expressed, I needed to know this guy was for real and not some false prophet, could I really believe, without proof.

Finally he moved in front of me again, this time I reached out to pass a letter I'd written. The palpitations of that moment nearly made me keel over but instead of taking my letter he took the one from the guy behind me before moving away to another part of the Mandera. There was no acknowledgment, not even a glance, feeling deflated I pondered my experience until it turned to hunger. It had been nearly two day's rather than try to dissect the mornings happening food gave me something else to focus on, starving I needed some.

. Leaving the Mandera Zonk lead me to the Western canteen where my fears about surviving on rice diminished. The variety and choice of dishes was amazing. Unaware of the affects of not eating, I greedily filled my tray with toasts, porridge, fruit and drinks. Half way through stuffing my face, my stomach began to reject the food to the point I wanted to throw up. Pushing my tray away I was happy to leave the rest of my breakfast, until my eye caught a large sign stating. 'Eat what you take, do not waste.'

Feeling bad I headed back to the dorm where I allow my stomach to settle. While there on the tattered mattress I drift into a day dream state. Images of Emma, how we met and thoughts of what she might be doing followed. Waking suddenly in a cold sweat I momentarily forgot where I was. Sitting next to me, was my Indian guardian. Smiling at me he asked my opinion on my Darsham. I explained my experiences alongside my disappointments.

"Swami gives us what we need, never underestimate Darsham." His words gave me hope, perhaps I didn't have to be aware of my significance at the Ashram right now, but my soul would be benefited, I comforted myself with the idea.

For the next three days I settled into daily life at the Ashram until the fourth day when it became hectic and thousands of new comers flowed through the gates for the birthday celebrations. Witnessing the absolute chaos taking place, me and Zonk decided to head for the meditation garden for some quiet time. After an hour's meditation Zonk turned to face me. "How did you get to hear about swami?"

"I've always had a fascination about the bigger picture in life. There's this knowing, that there's something far greater than my existence at work." Zonk was keen to comment and smiled. "Like swami tells us, we are all part of it."

"To me Zonk, it reminds me a little of the film star wars, the concept of an all powerful force that exists in all things, and in answer to your question of how I ended up here, let me explain. About six years ago, my life as I knew it was ripped away and no matter how hard I wanted things to work, it was like trying to hold sand in a sieve. My family was torn apart after my father died, funny really, you don't realise the importance of holding together the fragile idea of family, until they're gone. Not realising my own selfish nature and the continued search for ever more exterior pleasures. I used my self pity to propel me down a path that I knew in my heart was wrong, until I managed to destroy a lot of the people and the things that mattered to me. I was in love, but I allowed my ego to blind me to a very precious soul until she was gone. Depression set in on the inside, until the flickering spark of light in my heart nearly went out. Then one day, someone told me that I was special and that I was loved. Hearing these words ignited the fire once more in my soul, setting me off again, on a new path which has slowly brought me to this place."

Zonk sat quietly perhaps digesting my story until I broke the silence.

"So, how did you end up here?" Before speaking, he smiled calmly at me.

"I too lost my family in a car crash, I am the sole survivor." Zonk's comments made me feel selfish and full of self pity about my own story. Sure I felt I'd had it hard, but this guy had lost his entire family. "Zonk I'm so sorry, compared to my story I feel a little embarrassed. Jesus its time I put my story to bed." Inwardly I was feeling very worthless, igniting thoughts of, had I just played a poor me over my own problems.

"Jason, your experience was as real as mine. We are not only given what we need, but what we can handle. Do not judge yourself against others experiences, yes what happened to me was bad and put me on my path too but yours is also valid for it lead you to India." Zonks comments shocked me at first, how could he compare the two? "Please Jason, except what you felt as real, as real as mine or anyone else alive."

A strange empty feeling came over me followed by a rush of spirit. If he could accept my story then so could I, perhaps we really were only given what we could handle.

"Thank you." I said. "You're a special person." my comment resonated from my heart and I rejoiced in the fact. By the time I arrived back at our dorm, the heavens had opened and the rain begun to pelt down on the tin roof. Inside a goony looking guy was cooking vegetables on a stove and had quite a gathering of onlookers surrounding him, tuning into the happy vibe surrounding him I moved close enough to listen to what he was saying. "Water, I tell you it's all you need nothing else, it will heal anything." He spoke sternly and confidently his comment totally intrigued me.

"What about juices, milk and other forms?" A young Indian guy asked.

"No water is all you need, drink enough and you'll never be unwell." I was captivated by the warm vibe his enthusiasm generated. He had a very organic feel about him and seemed full of contentment. "No more fizzy drinks for me, then." The same Indian jested.

"Poison, absolute poison, there's enough sugar in that stuff to shut your immune system down for hours." The old man's comments made me aware of how little I knew about my body and also the effects of food and drink. He commented on meat and how it harboured negative energies and how it held no spiritual value what so ever. Strangely I hadn't eaten meat all week perhaps I thought, it was another area for me to evolve in. I sat for another half hour happy to listen to his views on the human body before moving back to my mattress where I lay back and listened to the rain combined with people laughing, the two sounds helped me slip into a semi conscious haze, a true feeling of peace washed over me, the kind of peace I only remember having as a child.

Having become accustomed to waking early, 4pm was no longer a problem. After a cold shower, I sat quietly in the dorm the thought of going home the next day plagued me. Part of me now knew I was ready for travelling but this was not the time to go walk about, I knew I had to return to England.

Morning Dasham flowed well into the afternoon and then a pleasant evening which I spent talking to my new- found friends one final time. The morning came round faster than usual I agreed to share a cab back to Bangalore with Zonk who was also leaving. My Indian guardian escorted us out of the village to the taxi hut.

"So has your trip been good?" He asked before leaving us.

"Yes" I replied, "and I'm so grateful for the help you've given me."

"We'll meet again, you'll see." Waving I watched him disappear. Driving to the airport a real sense of sadness and optimism washed over me...
Arriving at the terminal, Zonk insisted we share a beer. Expressing how impressed he had been

with some of my drawings over the past week, he asked if I could draw a portrait of him before I left, in exchange he would write a message in my diary. I waited till we'd said our goodbyes and Zonk had departed before I read it.

'Dear Jason,

Always remember, if you hold the strings to strong they might break and if you hold the strings to weak you are not able to play them, so find the golden middle way and you are able to, yours Zonk.'

His words were welcome, but I still had six hours to pass before I flew. In an attempt to relax I pulled out a book, but found it tough going. Putting it down I noticed a pretty young western girl about my age sitting opposite me. Feeling bold I went over and sat next to her and introduced myself. Turned out she was a French Canadian on her way to London, we hit it off straight away and slowly the evening passed. She had this tremendous energy for life, infectious it lifted my own spirits.

Midnight, moments before boarding she shared a piece of music with me. Both listening via ear plug to a flower duet from 'Lakme' it was a beautiful moment in which I felt content. Once we landed in England I kind of knew I'd never see her again, but that beautiful moment has never left me.

Collecting me from the airport I returned to Nat's. He had cooked some snacks some of which were chicken portions. Seeing the look on my face Nat grinned. "I've cooked it now, you can go veggie tomorrow."

I knew the first steps of change had arrived, but I needed more. All too quickly I was back at the works on the afternoon shift and my incredible journey was over. It was around nine that evening with only half an hour to go that I sat sipping some black coffee from the machine while smoking a roll up from old tobacco. When late the work shop had a surreal feeling, thinking of India I melt into it.

India had been everything I wanted it to be, I was still unsure of Sai Baba, but in my heart I now knew this being was not evil in any way. Maybe I hadn't experienced total bliss in his presence or got the personal interview I'd craved, but the experiences at the Ashram were laden with energy. My final entry into my diary during the trip had been about two thoughts, self worth and guilt. It would be months before the true understanding of what these thoughts had to do with me materialised, but the seeds were sewn it was now a case of how I could build on India.

Chapter 13

New Horizons

Saturday morning I was sat at my art desk studying a map of the world I'd recently acquired, when the phone began to ring. Debating whether I could be bothered to pick it up or not I allowed it to ring several times before casually answering it. "Hello is that Jay." To my surprise it was Jan.
"Hello Jan, how are you?"
"Fine, fine how was your trip to India?"
"Brilliant."
For the next ten minutes I relished the opportunity to talk about my trip as I hadn't really been given the chance to express my experience to anyone. Towards the end of the conversation, Jan told me about a new meditation group she was running every Monday night and that her intuition had told her that I may be interested. "That's really weird Jan, I was only thinking the other night about what steps I could take to build on India." Reminding me, nothings weird and that everything is meant Jan left me on a positive note. . Putting the phone down, I sensed a feeling of something good on the horizon, but what!

In the lead up to Christmas I attended Jan's group on a couple of occasions, it was just like old times only I now felt more prepared. It was during the last meditation session before Christmas, Jan told me about another source of energy she had recently discovered. "It's called Reiki Jay and I think it will be right up your street, In the New Year you ought to come along. We've got what's called a Reiki share running every Tuesday come and experience it, it's something we've all been looking for." J

Jan certainly had me intrigued; and things once more seemed to be moving with a purpose.

It was during the Christmas period my brother Dan came home unexpectedly from one of his adventures, this time France. He'd been gone for six months on a kind of fishing trip and had fallen for this French girl who happened to be dating one of his new found French friends, deciding she was the one they had got it together. Typical of Dan really, he had a knack of getting women to fall in love with him only to realise they weren't for him. Sitting down with him I tried to speak some sense with him.

"I don't understand you wrote letters. I thought you loved this one?"

"She's fucking mental mate properly, mad."

"Well what about her ex boyfriend this Cedric, guy weren't you ever worried about him?"

"What some jumped up little French neck, I'll smash his face in Jay."

"But weren't he in the army?"

"Like I said Jay, he's nothing." His comments didn't surprise he was rude about almost everything. Having rented his downstairs flat to Bill before going I quizzed him on his return plans. "I'm gonna stay with Mel and pork belly a while." His reply was flippant. Wondering how long that would last I left him to it and went back upstairs.

Pork belly was one of the many names Dan had given to my sister's husband. His real name was Allah and when they got together they loved nothing more than to compete against one another over everything and anything, if it wasn't clothes it was cash or cars eating or drinking rights, to who was richer fitter or faster than the other, right down to the beer they drank.

Christmas turned out to be a welcome break; I still very much enjoyed the whole experience of family, good food and time to relax. It was January I found dark and dreary, but this time I had something to look forward to, the Reiki.

The January blues weren't so bad I found picking up the trail from the previous year easy and head for the Reiki share now held in the rooms we had used for meditation. Entering the building, I was greeted by a little old lady who waited for me to remove my shoes, after she lead me to the Reiki room where a couple of people were laid on massage couches, others standing nearby laid their hands on different parts of the body, though the scene was one of quiet contemplation I began to feel a little shy and nervous until greeted by a friendly grey haired guy.

"Is this your first visit?" He whispered in my ear.

"Yes, what's this Reiki like?"

"Very good, just try and relax." Drawing away from the whispering, I closed my eyes and breathed slowly in an effort to do so. It wasn't long before I was on one of the beds. Closing my eyes I slowly began to let go. I must have laid there a good twenty minutes, before I became aware they'd removed their hands and that things were finished. Stirring gently I opened my eyes to Jan who was present, smiling she passed me a beaker of water. "How did you find it?"

"I'm not sure, really." I said.

"That's okay you took on a lot of energy, keep coming for a few weeks then see what you make of it." Jan's words were always a source of comfort. I returned over the next fortnight, and began to relax more and more until slowly I began to reach states similar to that of which I'd experienced in meditation. Regular attendance of the Reiki along with my meditation had never felt so right. Not since Jan's first group all those years ago had I felt so committed to something that benefited my spiritual growth. As the seeds of positive change began to once more sprout so did other challenging choices, choices that meant I would either flow with life or fight with life were about to arise.

"I'm gonna have to kick Bill out Jay, I need somewhere to live." Dan's comments weren't really a shock to me as I had a feeling it was only a matter of time. Regularly he'd expressed to me that living with Allah and Mel was far too tense. Hence forgetting the parts he probably played in it all. I felt for Bill, but I suppose he too must have known it was inevitable where Dan was concerned.

It was while fishing at the weekend with Allah that the conversation gave me an idea.

"So Jay you still going to go travelling?"

"Defiantly, I just need to get some money together."

"What about your job at the works?"

"Personally I get the feeling that its run course."

"Don't suppose you fancy coming to work for me and Mel, do ya?" Allah's gesture seemed a bit off the cuff so I didn't pay it too much attention at first, but he persisted.

"Since me and Mel bought those new moulds the business is on the verge of taking off, we're going to need someone for sure, Dan's been doing a few days a week while he lives at ours, but come spring Mel reckons it'll go mad."

"If you don't mind mate can I give it some thought?" With that I casually passed it off. That night I looked around my flat. It had taken me three years to get it just how I wanted, especially with the addition of my art room. But something was telling me, if you're going travelling wouldn't it be unfair to allow Dan to kick Bill out, the more I thought about it the more it bothered me so I decided to meditate upon it.

Once calm and centred I induced my high c to merge with me until I felt at one, then I laid down my situation and waited for a reply.

"Jason you will travel let go of the flat and follow your dreams."

"But where will I live, and how will I get the money together."

"Trust in the universe, take the job with Allah and Mel, you're needed there. The rest will happen if you learn to let go." Coming out of my meditation, my desire to follow my high c was strong, venturing down stairs on a bit of a high, I intended to tell Bill of my plans but as I slowly got stoned with him my old demons returned. "You don't want to travel." My ego kept telling me. "Why should you give up your cosy flat for him?" After an hour of mental torture, I got up and looked at Bill.

"Why the hell do I still smoke this shit!" As I left the room Bill just laughed, I could still hear him on reaching the upstairs flat. As it turned out the evening served as a positive, to spite the weed I rang Dan that morning and told him my plan.

Surprisingly he seemed quite upbeat and supportive of the whole idea, telling me he admired my decision. Next stop was over to Allah's. Mel seemed over the moon with the whole idea. "You can have the spare room Dan's been using. Plus if you work for us there will be no rent to pay."

"That's that sorted then. I'll move in the end of March."

"Come out here Jay I'll show you a few bits while your here."

Taking me into the garden where the business was based Allah showed me what was what. I was thoroughly impressed with their industry, Mel had come up with all sorts of new finishes for the statues and they looked superb. Being at the beginning of something ready to grow I began to feel excited. Stopping at the end of the garden I gasped. "Jesus Allah, what happened to this lot?" The pile of deformed ornaments stacked up was hideous. Headless animal's, bloated statues and planters that looked like someone had peppered them with a machine gun were stacked high.

"That's Dan's creation he doesn't listen, thinks he can take short cuts and that's the result."

"Sounds about right, how come you aint got rid of them?"

"Apparently he wants 'em Jay, says he's going to build a freak show in the back garden, at his place."

"Now why doesn't that surprise me?"

That night in the flat I contemplated my time at the works an immense gratitude weld up for the place, I knew deep down I hadn't always given it my best, and that I'd played the fool too many times, but I felt quite proud to have worked there. Graham my team leader was a good man and someone I respected so I decided to hold out on my notice a further few weeks. A knock on the downstairs door drew my attention hearing Dan's voice I made a cup of tea and ventured down to see him and Bill. Entering the kitchen his usual unsavoury humour hit me.

"Hello boy, Jertsie here!" Like Baz, Dan enjoyed mimicking film quotes himself.

"Dan tells me you're moving out to your sisters?" Bill was quick to ask.

"Yeah well…. it makes sense for everyone involved."

"Nice one Jay." Bills voice was full of gratitude, unlike the sarcastic and uncouth comments that flowed from Dan's mouth.

"Yeah, nice one shmice one!" His sarcasm was stifling at times. "Jay's going to play peaceful warrior to Allah and Sister Mel."

"I'll be alright. I'll help them, and they'll help me."

"I'm sure you will boy, what help yourself to some of Allah's arse, when he's on the whisky." Dan just couldn't help but be rude and crude.

"Leave it out Dan." Bill defended. "Leave your brother alone."

"Shut up Bill or is it pet chimp, your days are numbered, you and all your sick buddies." Sensing Dan's bullish mood I was keen to get back to my flat.

 Concluding my day in my diary that night life felt good, I was pleased with my commitment to the flow of life, the great explorer within was once again soaring.

Chapter 14

Letting Go

As March roared into April it was time to move. Clearing out and packing things up from my flat I was amazed at how much surplus junk and sentimental baggage I had accumulated. Mel and Allah had assured me there was plenty of space in their loft for storage so it wasn't a huge problem but still a trip to the dump and charity shop was needed to offload at least a dozen black bags of stuff I no longer used.

Entering the charity shop I was surprised to be told that they didn't need any of the things I had. Wondering what to do with it all I stood a moment outside the shop on Newport high street, while standing there a familiar face approached. "Hello Jay." An old mate from school I hadn't seen Sarah for ages.

"Alright Sarah, how are you? Pretty freaky bumping into you, it was only the other day I found out your dad's my team leader at the works."

"I know. I couldn't believe it when he said you were working there, and I know what you're like Jason, so I hope you are behaving yourself." Still laughing we spent the next ten minutes catching up on old times before both departing in different directions. What a peculiar coincidence Sarah's dad being my ex boss I thought, then walking away I quickly remembered that there is no such thing as a coincidence.

The next day Allah came round to help me move the rest of my things to his house. Unlike the flat I'd just come from the homely feeling was infectious making me feel child like once more. The first evening in my little room at Mel and Allah's was serenely peaceful.

Over the next week, Allah showed me the ropes in the garden casting and stripping the moulds they used to make garden ornaments. I was thoroughly impressed by my sisters industry and enthusiasm to the small self built business. It was good to be at the beginning of something I could sense was going to take off.

"You'll see." She said "Well be as big as Disney in a couple of years."

I'll give Mel her credit she was never afraid to reach for the stars. With spring in the air the light nights were upon us bringing also mid week football matches. It was prior to one of these matches I was about to learn a valuable lesson, on their way out Mel and Allah were leaving me to it for the first time.

"So, you know what you're doing?" Mel fussed. "Sure you'll be alright."

"You just go and enjoy yourselves."

Waving them away I shut the door. I'd been given the responsibility of mixing and casting alone all afternoon, five mixes was my target for the day.

Now a mix consists of about thirteen shovel loads of ballast, half a bag of cement, a full cap of black dye, brought to just the right consistency in the mixer. Then the loading process, into the varied sized moulds, to finish, they were then banged and shook vigorously to remove any air bubbles, apparently a lot of Dan's mistakes had come about by wet mixes, and what Allah described as a touch of laziness.

I was doing well but by the fourth mix I began to tire, looking to the clock I saw it said four thirty pm, I had to meet the team at five thirty for a six o'clock kick off, knowing a mix took around half hour to complete and that there were two left I paused. Resting a moment I began to contemplate not bothering, I'm sure Allah would understand I thought. Then taking three deep breaths I asked my high c to help me summon the strength or give me a solution.

"Work from your heart." Popped in my head, but how does one physicalize that idea I thought. "You know," came an answer. Slowly I began to fill the mixer and with each shovel full I told myself 'work from your heart'. Positive thoughts of my sister and Allah succeeding began to materialise in my head, so I continued to purposely chant, 'Work from your heart,' until it became like a mantra. Soon my strength began to return until nothing mattered but giving my best, as if the future of the business depended on it I poured love into my work. An immense gratitude pulsed through me, mentally in the moment I felt physically strong, alive, and emotionally immersed in love...As if time had stood still the following two mixes were the most fulfilling work I'd ever done and I was down the football pitch for five thirty just as the nets went up. The game itself was not only the last of the season but it would be the last in a Crawley shirt for all of us, after six years together the team had run its course and we went out on a high winning six nil.

Inside the pub afterwards 'here's where the story ends' played out loud. Taking myself and my drink to one side I had to acknowledge that it was truly the end of an era. Lifting me from my indulgent thoughts Jock joined me and begun voicing off.

"I hear you're going travelling Jay?"

"Yep, it's got to happen, this is my year."

"Fancy some company on your travels?"

"Why do you fancy it then?"

"Well I got nothing holding me back." Thinking it was just another of Jocks fanciful whims I took his comments tongue in cheek. But as we talked, it became apparent that he was serious, knowing it could be a laugh the thought of a companion grew appealing. "Look Jock I'm going whatever, but if you do fancy it, brilliant."

"Oh I'm bang up for it mate, I know your probably thinking I'll fall in love with some bird and won't come, but it's different in my life now, I feel I really need this." Jock's comments came across pretty sincere prompting a response of my own.

 "You got no worries there mate, I'm no longer looking for love, I feel I've finally let go." As the comment loosely flowed out, a sense of knowing also surrounded it. What had seemed at first just a polite return to Jock's gesture hit me with a sense of certainty. I really meant it, for nearly six years I'd searched and wanted a new love after Emma, but to no avail. What now seemed a bizarre search had come to an end?

Writing in my diary that night, I was beginning to feel as though part of my youth was concluding. This thought came with some uneasy feelings, like a sense of loss. But before I allowed my overactive mind to bring my energies into a state of anxiety, I was inspired by the thought that this was also a new beginning.

My regular visits to the Reiki saw a small community of light minded people spring up from and around the centre. Dinidi the grey haired guy I'd met on the first night never missed a session then there was Jen a Reiki master and Penny the Kinisiologist who worked and ran the shop out front. During a meditation session one week I chose my brother Dan to do a tie cutting with, it brought about profound and unexpected results; I noticed a new closeness begin to blossom between us but without the bullshit. It was after one of these energising meditations that Jan informed me of a trip to India.

"I'm so excited Jay, yet so scared."

"Scared?" I quizzed her in surprise. Hoping my questioning wasn't leading to a long story I waited her reply. Talking to Jan was always positive, but sometimes she would go off on one for anything up to an hour.

"I hate flying Jay, its one of my big fears but Jimmy is organising a trip to the ashram." The sound of a plain drew our attention skyward. "You'll be fine." I assured her. "It'll be an amazing adventure."

I Know." She chuckled in one of her funny little laughs. "I'm sure some of the others will be supportive." It sounded like quite a few people were going. Driving home part of me felt a little left out, why no one had invited me. Rationalizing it I thought it maybe because people knew I was already going travelling, still it would have been nice to of been asked.

That night was to be the beginning of a series of dreams, some that included Emma, one of the more vivid I wrote in my diary. We'd found each other again in an uninterrupted fortnight of which we put all our old hurts behind us, sharing some magical moments. Only this time when we parted there was a sense of completion. Other dreams involved being in the pub and drinking with the lads till closing, when everyone went to leave I realised I was naked in my bed and unable to follow them out because I had no clothes. Yet everyone acted as though it was perfectly normal. Jan had always encouraged me to keep notes about dreams as they could hold keys to future events.

With the exception of being Nat's best man at his wedding, May flew by with summer in full swing, the garden ornaments grew like spring bulbs and business was booming allowing Mel and Allah to find new premises, giving them back there garden. Amongst it all, I'd spent quite a few Friday nights with Jock and made new plans for our travelling. Some weeks we'd go uptown for our drink, on the odd occasion Jock would pull a bird he was like a magnet to women how he managed it I'll never know! It was during one of these Fridays I began to doubt Jock's sincerity about travelling.

"You're come and visit us won't ya Pinchy?" Smiling smugly Jock drooled over the girl in question. "Anything for you Jocky." The girl giggled.

My main reason for travelling was born out of the need for adventure, along with a spiritual filled journey and I just wasn't sure if Jock was on the same wave length. My fears of travelling alone were once again creating a situation I could do without.

By mid June the world cup was well on its way, leading to an all weekend of five aside football... The tournament was to be held in the impressive new hockey stadium, it was a gorgeous day there were stalls, food areas and plenty of people preparing for the great atmosphere. For the event we were drawn out of the hat as Mexico. The name didn't faze me, unlike some of the other players.

"Mexico, bloody Mexico!" Rick wasn't impressed. "I mean who the fuck is Mexico." Rick was one of the craziest men you'd ever meet on a football pitch but he made us laugh. Jogging out for a light warm up I was pleased to see that Jock had turned up as I passed him he stopped me.

"There you are, man have I got some news I know your gonna love."

"Go on." Smiling I jogged on the spot.

"Your never gone believe who I saw last night, Jay."

"One of your many female admirers maybe?"

"Na, someone I know your gonna want to meet."

Jock's enthusiasm had my complete attention.

"Go on then before the game starts."

"Well I was up the swan last night usual crowd was out, pretty boring really, anyway I was about to leave when I got chatting to Emma, turns out she's single and would love to catch up with you."

His comment didn't register at first. "Emma, jay, come on there's only ever been one Emma." Then it hit me stunned I spoke.

"But we aint spoke a word in six years Jock."

"Well she wants to talk now mate, in fact she sounded really excited by the thought. She's over at her mothers; they're on holiday for a fortnight so she's there on her own."

"What and she actually said to call her."

"Yer man you know the number don't ya 812." Interrupting him I finished the number off, "how could I forget." Though Jock continued to talk about the conversation they had had, my mind was now elsewhere. This was a moment I'd longed for in my heart, a chance to find some form of completion with someone I'd loved, and had been unable to let go of. For the rest of the day between matches my mind was running different scenarios, what if she'd changed, perhaps she was drunk the night before, just ring her, be cool, find some peace of mind at last.

I'd recently told Jock I'd given up looking for love, was love now seeking me?

Before committing to a ring tone that night I must have dialled and hung up several times. Taking a deep breath I listened as the phone began to finally ring. Ending in the answer machine I found myself feeling awkward. Umm I thought to myself do I leave a message, before I had time to think I found myself scrambling one off, it was done I'd rolled the dice. Despite exceeding all our expectations of reaching the semi finals of football the day dragged. Not wanting to miss a phone call that evening decorating my room was a good excuse to stop in. Sure enough around eight thirty the telephone began to ring. Just by the pulse of my heart I knew it was Emma.

"Hello," I said bold as brass.

"It's Emma."

"Hello how are?"

"Fine, god this is weird after all these years."

"I know." The conversation flowed over trivial matters before we decided to meet up and catch up. "You do know that England are playing tomorrow night don't ya?

"Yeah that's okay." I cheekily replied. "I can watch it at yours."

"You haven't changed there, then, what about seven pm?"

"Sure I'll look forward to it."

Putting the phone down I was overwhelmed and feeling of excitement began to brew. Calm down I told myself it's just a get together. But I could feel I was struggling to hold back an avalanche of emotion, in fact I began to feel all over the place. Quickly I reminded myself of the journey I'd taken since she'd left. A path perhaps I may never have taken had we not parted. Breathing deeply I began to calm down, stay detached, be cool, it's only a get together I told myself again and again. Perhaps it was only my fear of rejection that held me back from admitting that I still loved her.

Chapter 15

The Moment

Monday at work was agonisingly slow. In between checking the time and filling the mixer rushes of excitement came over me. Finally stepping into the shower and singing like a crazed rocker I begun furiously scrubbing the black dye from my body. Deciding to peddle across town I grabbed my bike and got going. With the light evenings and summer air it gave me a chance to calm my thoughts, but as I pulled up into the street I'd grown up in, I had mixed feelings about the evening ahead. 'Detach.' I affirmed to myself. The garden hadn't changed a bit, parking my bike against the gate the door opened before I had a chance to knock, there she was.

"Alright, god you haven't changed a bit." I quickly expressed.

"Jesus, nor have you come in." Entering I felt confident, I'd worked hard on myself for six years and knew I wasn't the same teenager shed known back then. After a drink and some small talk, I also became aware that this wasn't the same Emma I'd known, but I could still feel the immense attraction I'd had, coming back. Her every action alongside everything she said seemed to be fuelling my passion for her. I felt urges to tell her I'd never stopped loving her, and how she'd been the inspiration behind a lot of my successes, but I held back, keeping the conversation easy and light hearted. Deep inside I was saddened to hear that she had not made use of her immense talents in art or modelling, and even more surprised to discover the pattern of her working life was similar to that of my own drifting from job to job never really building a career. As the night bore on our conversations turned to our passions and dreams. I told her about my intentions to travel at the end of the year and was surprised to hear her tell me it was hers to.

A few more drinks and conversation took us to a point, where I sensed the energy was now firmly shifting towards a physical moment. We had total eyes for one another.

"Kiss me Jay."

"I'm not that easy." Holding back a moment I smiled and then it happened, all the rejection, hurt and pain, everything I'd experienced was washed away and replaced with an immense sense of love.

"Stay with me tonight."

"Yes" was all I said.

Leaving in the morning I was as light as a feather. Peddling down the red way I begun to laugh swing and swerve my bike from side to side. A cool summer shower only infused my mood all the more, punch drunk on love it was a moment I knew I had to savour. Arriving at work Allah was immediately on me with a huge grin. "Things went alright then last night Jay?"

"You could say that."

"Do I sense a bit of love in the air?"

"I'm not saying a word now crank up that mixer, and let's get these moulds filled."

Unlike the previous day, work flew by. And before I knew it I was back at Emma's.

"This feels so surreal being back here I honestly thought we'd never see each other again."

"Do you believe in fate, that your destiny is written in the stars?" Emma's question took me by surprise. The previous evening I'd held back about the spiritual side of my life. "I have a belief everything is meant good or bad, in fact most of our best moments were born out of bad situations, why do you ask?"

"When I thought about it today, you being here with me now, strange as it sounds hasn't come as a shock, over the last three month's I've actually received a lot of signs."

Intrigued I smiled. "Go on."

"Well it all started when I lived in the flat up town, I was drawing a picture of my Nan when I heard this strange voice in my head say 'He's outside.'. Whose outside? I thought. Then I had a strange mental vision of you, and let me tell you now, I hadn't thought about you for years. At first I thought 'nah.' Then the voice said it again. 'He's outside.' I put down my pad ran downstairs and opened the front door and who do I bump into but Sarah and I hadn't seen her for years either. She just looked at me and said. "Christ Emma you look like you just seen a ghost."

"Feels like it, I've just had a right mad moment where I thought of Jay, and that he was in town, silly, sad I know." I was feeling pretty stupid at this point when she said. "Oh how freaky is that. I've just had a conversation with him not two minutes ago outside the charity shop." Sarah's words left me compelled to grab my shoes and run out into the town to see if I could see you. I had no idea why I was doing it at the time."

"Wow I remember that day I met Sarah to." Feeling excited by the little bit of synchronicity I asked if there was anything else.

"Oh yes dreams. One in particular Jay, I was walking round an Indian market looking at silks and other material and you were with me. Oh my god I've just thought of something else as well." Excited by the way the conversation was flowing I urged her to carry on. Well about nine months ago someone paid for me to visit a clairvoyant and she told me all sorts of things one of which was that someone with the initials JD would sweep me of my feet and change my life. Again I didn't pay it too much attention as I couldn't think of anyone with the initials JD." I had never been a big fan of clairvoyants, but Emma's story certainly intrigued me.

"So you think I'm the man with the initial JD then do you?" Joking I sat back and took a deep breath. "Seriously Emma your story sounds pretty amazing."

I went on to tell Emma about my meetings at Jan's all those years ago, how I'd learnt to meditate and all about the Croatia trip. "A lot has changed in my life, and how I view the world As you can imagine, most of my friends find it all a bit much, Jay the crown prince looking for spiritual understanding, well I tell ya, I've experienced things that go beyond words. If I was to give weight to it, the word amazing would only ever be used once. That's how I'd describe my spiritual journey, amazing."

"Strange you telling me this, as since the turn of the year I too have had so many searching questions about what I'm doing here and what life's all about, feels like I've just opened my eyes for the first time."

Hearing this was music to my ears. Emma was perhaps the first girl I'd met who seemed ready to explore the idea that there was something bigger than us at work in the universe. Over the following few evenings deep conversation about life's miracle followed and I was able to express things I'd kept inside for too long.

"So who was the funny Indian guy with the afro in your wallet?" It was a question I knew sooner or later would come up. "He's what people refer to as a cosmic avatar, or spiritual master depending on which way you wish to interpret it, look I'm not one to devote life to a single idea, yet in the same breath I've learned not to close myself either, at the end of the day you have to trust yourself, that you know the difference between right and wrong. Sai Baba is very powerful in the way he talks about love, universal laws and how all religions and spiritual ideas lead back to the same source."

"Umm, I must admit I'm not a big religious fan, from my prospective they just seem to cause wars."

"I agree, but Sai Baba is not what I'd call a religion, it's more a lesson in self awareness about who we are, and how everything must come from us, from within our soul and heart, and to stop looking for some exterior source such as religion or wealth to meet our needs or answers."

"Ok, I'm cool with that."

Changing the subject I asked Emma how long we had the house for before her mum returned. She told me her mother wasn't due back for a further two weeks giving us plenty of time to catch up."

. That night as Emma dozed off, I lay in a state of peace this was everything I'd ever hoped for there was a magic in the air and a high I never wanted to end. I felt as though I'd been in a training school for the past six years preparing for something bigger and with Emma at my side the possibilities seemed boundless. Feeling high I was very happy to just drift in and out of consciousness until morning.

Waking I was reminded of a dream in which we had assured one another of our love before once again parting. Pondering over this my growing attachments became apparent, like in the movies I wanted more, a happy ever after and surely it had

to be Emma. Then it hit me what if she didn't feel the same. Appearing in the doorway she smiled. "Here you go Jay a nice cuppa."
As she settled back in bed I drew strength from the idea that it was better to know how we both felt now than be let down later.
"Emma do you remember when we were younger, I mean I know a lot happened between us, but you do realise I loved you and have never been able to let go of that love. Even after we split it somehow strengthened me in ways that now seeing you again are only just becoming apparent. I know we've only seen each other a week but I can't hide it the fact I still."
"shhhhhhhh. I feel the same theirs only ever been one man in my heart and that is you."
"Then come travelling with me, you said yourself that was your main goal this year, perhaps that's why we have met now and not before."
"Ok let's do it." Hearing those words lifted me, I felt the whole universe was with us and couldn't believe my luck. Then I remembered that when things are good challenge the universe that they get better.
"On the subject of travel Em, let me tell you another wonder I've discovered, the mountains, oh you'd love them in fact let me show you this weekend lets go to Edinburgh then onto the mountains. Its stunning and you'll love Edinburgh."
Emma's expression told me all I needed to know. Luckily for me I knew Edinburgh well, Dug had moved there on a rolling contract earlier that year

giving me and Dan the chance to make few visits. The rest of the week flew by everything was arranged with Dug and we were ready to leave.

Being the more reliable of the two vehicles we decided to take Emma's car but I got the feeling she was very protective over her vehicle. The journey was alright to begin with but as night fell the motorways became a living hell, cue after cue of cars had accumulated causing the longest of traffic jams. Once we reached the A1 I pulled over and pushed the seats back I was knackered so it didn't take long for me to fall asleep.

A poking finger woke me from what seemed like little sleep.

"Jay, wake up."

"What's up?"

"Check out the sun rise." Rubbing my eyes I wearily sat up. Lifting my head I became aware of my scenery and surroundings. It was nothing spectacular other than rolling fields with a low lying mist but my energies quickly lifted. There was something romantic about sharing the rising orange sun on a romantic journey with someone you loved.

Rolling into town around six we stopped at Dugs for an early morning visit. Good to his word Dug had sorted out a bed and breakfast along with a reservation at a nice restaurant. It was around nine that we wandered into the town centre, the main boulevard highlighted the city and its stunning views making it all quite apparent.

"What do ya think then?"

"It's amazing jay."

"I knew you'd like it, c'mon we got loads to see."

Holding hands we strolled along pushing and pulling and genuinely being silly. An Art gallery gave way to spectacular views of the castle, ice creams in the park, along with time to talk about hero's and idles of life." "Fancy lunch in one of the little cafe's Jay?"

"I've got a better idea; c'mon you're going to love it."

"What?"

"You'll see, first we need some supplies." Picking up some goodies from the local supermarket, I was intent on finding Cranock bay, a picturesque sea village with its own accessible island when the tide was out. Remembering how to get there, I figured might pose a few problems, but today the force was with me and a mixture of memory hunches soon lead us down into the pub car park in Cranock.

"God it's beautiful." Grabbing our food bag I teased Emma before running off.

"Let's get going before the tide comes in." I yelled back at her. Following we found the trip across the bay didn't take long finding a perfect picnic spot we settled down on a quiet part of the Island. Looking up from her food Emma smiled.

"Today's just been amazing Jay and it seems to just get better and better."

"I thought you might like it, try and take in as much scenery as you can."

"Everything's happened so fast over the last two weeks I still can't believe it's all really real."

"I know." I replied. "Its ironic like everything hasn't had a chance to catch up with itself. For nearly six years I tried to find love again. With the exception of one girl it wasn't until recently I finally realised I'd given up looking for love, then you came back into my life. I suppose its like Jan once told me, if you love someone let them go, if they come back they're yours, if they don't they never were."

A moments silence followed before Emma asked. "So who was this other girl, then?"

"Lisa, she was great but it just didn't work out. I guess I allowed my ego to get in the way somewhat, but I'm thankful to her and I wonder if she'll ever know how much she did help me."

"Oh, yeah," Emma said sarcastically.

"C'mon eat up." I said changing the subject. "We still got plenty to still see."

Finishing our lunch we paddled playfully in and out of the oncoming surf, heading back we soaked one another with it. The B and B had little to offer in the way of thrills but the views however were spectacular, reaching over Edinburgh the city lights allowed its full beauty to shine. Following dinner that night we sat on our bedroom window ledge watching the lights while talking travel and dreams. No longer watching a movie I was now living my own.

Our trip the following day to Lock Katrina was the perfect conclusion to what had to be a magical experience. Driving north that morning, warmth had returned to my heart. I was now beginning to understand some of the universal truths that had only been mere words until now. They were now feelings I understood but could not put words to. Making our way around the lock I led us up and off the well trodden tracks. Light showers gave way to rays of light that lit up the wonderful colours of the hill side. Asking me where I was going Emma questioned me. Smiling I told her to simply enjoy the scene unfolding before us. Gradually it grew more and more spectacular. Finally descending a little I spied the spot I'd been looking for, a small rock outcrop that looked reasonably excisable. Scrambling up, a strange sense of destiny came over me. Pulling Emma upward I smiled.

"Oh wow jay this is just breath taking." Acknowledging her the scene took on a whole new meaning "Em, I know this is gonna sound freaky, but over there to our left doesn't it feel familiar?"

"Oh my god, it's the painting hanging in your front room, the one your dad did...All that's missing is the stag from the clearing. As she spoke all the hairs on my body tingled and stood on end."

"Would you like to meditate for a while?" I asked her. Closing our eyes, silence followed breathing slowly a while I could sense my soul, then.

"Jay, Jay there's something down there." Emma's comments sounded frightening snapping me back to reality. Looking in the direction of movement I too became alarmed. The tall fern trees and undergrowth were moving as if a large animal was pushing through them. "Hold still." I whispered. My heart was now racing, for barely ten metres in front of us something large was about to emerge.

"Oh my god," Emma's words didn't do justice to the picture in front of us, there as if to complete the portrait was the prince of the forest.

At first we both gazed in ore of the mighty stag staring proudly at us, its regal poise beautiful beneath the sun before it turned and trotted off.

"Seeing that scene reminds me of something your dad said to me once, he told me you'd never be anything till you got out of Newport, he also asked me if I'd look out for you, as you needed looking after, that was the last time I saw your dad."

"Perhaps seeing that was a sign for you Emma, along with a timely reminder to me of how much you meant to me during our years apart. You were there, inspiring me on to better things, as if by some chance you may notice the light in me once again." Turning to her I smiled. "Thank you."

It was a weekend to always be treasured.

Chapter 16

Into The Sun Set

The rest of the summer was a blend of hard work and car boot sales to fund our trip away. Long hot summer days gave way to cooler autumn air and a return of shorter nights, along with the strange haunting September feeling that I just couldn't put my finger on.

Our leaving date was November the 28th Emma had agreed to visit Baba's ashram with the group Jimmy had put together, comfortable with the idea I hoped it would ease us into our journey. The shortfall in cash became more apparent as we moved into October helping us to make the decision to sell up everything of value. After sorting through all my stuff at home we then moved onto Emma's messy room.

"Here, Em, Halloweens just round the corner someone might buy these." Crawling out from under her bed I held up a pair of dusty old socks. "Ha Ha it happens." She smirked.

"How you survived so long in this tiny box room, I'll never know." Ignoring my comment she continued her relentless cleaning pursuit then slowly she looked over her shoulder. "Here's something you might remember." She passed me a small paper envelope, curiously I looked inside. "Oh my god, it's the pearl I brought you back from America, you kept it."

. "Of course, why wouldn't I." Passing it back I watched carefully where she placed it. That night while she made tea I took it out, seeing it again had given me an idea for her birthday. Getting permission from her mum to stay over I put my plan together.

Waking up Early I slipped down stairs filling a tray with fresh fruit, porridge juice and toast I placed the small present beside a rose and carried it all up to her.

"Hey up, someone's been busy."

"If, we pretend, who knows, this could be Paris." I held back on the present while we ate, then taking the tray away I gave it to her.

"Oh jay it's beautiful, when did you do this?"

"Let's just say I thought it appropriate."

Taking the pearl I'd set in gold from her I did it up around her neck.

"I love you Jay."

"I know." Turning away to pour the tea, I asked Emma if she was nervous about our trip.

"Yeah, I'd be lying if I said no. Why?"

"I don't know really, did I tell you Jan isn't coming now?"

"No." Surprised Emma sat up. "When did she decide this?"

"Last meditation night I went to, looks as though her fear of flying just got the better of her."

"Poor Jan, you did say we all have our fears to overcome?"

125

"Given her knowledge I thought she would have trusted a little more in the universe, after all it was Jan that introduced me to the affirmation. 'Feel the fear and do it anyway."

"I'll have to remind you of that one the next time your scared." With a touch of sarcasm Emma smiled.

"By the way a few of the lads want to have a good bye drink if you fancy it?"

"Yes that could be nice." With family all wanting to give us farewell dinners the weeks before our departure were busier than we had imagined them to be. In amongst it the final preparations with only days to go, Emma decided and managed to sell her car. With lots of friends present our farewell drink in the pub turned into a party of emotions. Feeling as thou I'd climbed a high summit on a distant peak bathed in sunshine, I immersed myself in the feeling I'd come full circle. Then a strange sobering thought came over me it had taken best part of six years, this thought was followed by a sadness the kind you get when you know something is about to end. Surely this is the beginning I told myself, looking around the room watching the people I'd grown up with smile and laugh, more strange feelings arose.

Feeling like something was about to leave my life, I was snapped from my inner world.

"Come on jay, group photo." Bills smiling face brought back a sense of belonging and friendship and a warm feeling resided, things were gonna be good.

The heat coupled with the strange bitter sweet smell of India filtered through my senses; I was back only this time not alone. Driving to the ashram Jimmy told stories about it to Emma. Quietly I observed the arid landscape. A mixture of staying head strong on the outside gave way to the odd bouts of inward anxiety over what may lay ahead. Completely embracing the moment along with Jimmy's stories Emma showed no signs of nerves. "Did you visit the fulfilling wish tree the last time you were here Jay?"

Yes." I replied "it's a beautiful setting." Jimmy went on to tell Emma of the fruits Sai Baba sometimes picked from the tree at the request of the people. "What any fruit?"

"So we're told." Jimmy continued. "These days' people go down and hang written wishes all over it." Emma smiled she seemed so acceptant of Baba and his ashram along with the many miracles that happened. I'd known now of Baba for over five years and yet a part of me still held back just trust your heart I told myself.

Arriving I was surprised to discover that we would be staying in male, female dorms, after a long wait with the accommodation officer I finally entered a room with Jimmy. Putting his stuff down Jimmy stood straight. "Right I'm off out into the village for supplies and to locate this Aurevidic clinic I've heard about."

Nodding I lay back on the mattress and fell into a strange dream where I was the conductor of a large musical orchestra, only the people that played were all people I knew from home.

The sound of knocking brought me round, opening the door I saw a weary looking well groomed Indian guy stood before me. "My name is Ray. They tell me you have space for another in this room."

"Well there are only two beds." Knowing this the thought of another troubled me.

"Of course, I don't want to be any bother." Then my heart opened to the weary looking traveller. "Come in I'm sure we can make room."

"Oh thank you my brother, this is most kind." I watched him settle into the room with very little dialogue. Returning Jimmy brought some people with him. "David, this is Jason."

I got the feeling Jimmy already knew David by the way they talked. "And this is Vishal." Jimmy continued. "These guys are staying at the ashram, so I thought we may meet up in the mornings for Darsham."

"Okay." I said. "Cool by me." Two others entered to chat to Jimmy so Vishal turned to me.

"So Swami has called you to him?"

"Yep, I have heard it put this way before, and you?"

"Oh yes, he has much work for me, I am his humble servant. So Jason, what do you hope to gain from this visit?"

"Understanding balance, umm do you know I haven't really come here with any expectations."

My response seemed to startle vishal. "Perhaps it's to open your heart young man."

"And how does one do that?"

"It is like riding a bike; once you get it you never forget it."

"Yeah, but how does one learn to ride the bike in the first place?"

Vishal laughed openly "by trusting in God my friend." More riddles I thought as they all prepared to leave the dorm. Agreeing to meet the others in the morning I settled back on my bed. Jimmy soon began talking to Ray; it was the first time he had spoken properly since arriving. "My journey here on the train was awful." He said. "At first there is room, but then more brothers come on train I make room but they keep coming with every stop until I cannot move. Now I feel crushed I see my stop but cannot get of, oh it was horrible."

"So where did you come from, and what about your family." Jimmy asked. "Do you have a wife?"

"Everywhere I go she watch me, we go to super market I look at the floor in fear she may attack me."

"How do you feel about this?"

"Oh I feel so cocooned Jimmy."

"Do you think she's crazy?"

"I dun no, I dun no?" Inwardly a strange thing began to occur; I could sense laughter, uncontrollable laughter ready to explode. At first I tried to hide it due to sheer embarrassment, here was a guy pouring out his heart and I was ready to explode with laughter, what was going on. Pulling the sheet over my head I bit down hard on my lip till the feeling gave way to sleep, peaceful sleep.

As agreed we all met up for morning Darsham, while Jimmy begun one of his expansive conversations with Vishal I got to know our new room mate who had decided to join the small group that had formed.

"Do you know where the aurevedic clinic is?"I asked him.

"Yes aurevedic clinic in the village, I can show you."

"Well it's not really for me." I replied in a weary fashion. "It's Jimmy, in not sure what it's all about really."

"I take both of you; it's very good for body and soul, good medicine good massage." Ray continued to tell me about the benefits as we queued, but I found myself struggling to stay with him. The morning Darsham was just as I remembered it, a long wait followed by a wondrous curiosity about Sai Baba. One thing it had begun to teach me was that part of his example was to be the example.

Over breakfast I told Jimmy that Ray knew where the aurevidic clinic was.

"That's good, yeah good." His answer seemed distant, like his mind was elsewhere.

"You alright mate?"

"Fine, maybe I guessed or expected some sort of acknowledgement from Baba." Again his comments surprised me I'd always thought he had a firm understanding of all spiritual matters. Leaving the canteen we met up with Ray who was eager to show us where the aurevedic clinic was, following him into the village he left us at the entrance of it. The inside of it was not how

I expected it to be, for some reason I had this run down doctor's surgery in my head. Instead it had a light fresh, very professional feel to it. We were shown to a consultation room where we were asked to wait. I allowed Jimmy to go first, relaxing back I tried to hear what the doctor was saying to him next door, Instead I found myself drifting into thoughts about Emma. Seeing her also venture into the village that morning had brought up ancient feelings I thought I had dealt with long ago. They revolved around the thought she had left me, or was planning to. Part of me challenged these feelings with, 'I'm detached, 'what will be will be' but it did nothing to quell the rising feeling that was beginning to gather pace. Returning Jimmy's presence didn't register at first then standing before me, he smiled a huge grin. "Sorry I was miles away, is it my turn?"

"And you sir, hello." The doctor gestured for me to follow him.

After some basic questions I explained about how I had given up smoking little over a week ago, and was feeling a bit run down. He decided after a good massage, I would require nasal treatment to help the nerve endings in my brain rebalance; after a quick talk I told him I was game. A few moments later he took me back to Jimmy. "Ok, you guys come back at two o'clock today." Smiling he left us with time to kill.

The next few hours became a tense anxious affair, why was I experiencing these ancient feelings, where had they come from? Looking for distractions I ventured out for a stroll through the meditation garden. I needed to clear my head but it didn't happen.

"Hello Jay this place is amazing, I feel so free." Emma's comments frustrated me, she seemed so chilled out but I attempted to keep my cool.

"Yep it certainly is I see you've started sketching."

"Yeah, god it's been so long since I've done any, do you want to join me?"

"No, I've got some treatment in about twenty minutes but you carry on."

"Oh Jay, I'm so glad I came away. I'm so looking forward to travelling, I can see myself in Thai land chilling out, finding myself." Emma's excitement only fuelled my anxiety, and what did she mean, she could see her self in Thailand, where was I? A brief hug and we parted. Why were these thoughts plaguing me? Was this some test just to show how fragile I still was, or perhaps to show me how attached I had already become, and if I was not careful the same fate awaited me as before.

Ghosted in my own space, unaware of the pedlars, beggars and community of street folk who loved to talk I wandered on back to the clinic with a few moments to spare. Jimmy was already there reading one of the many books that could be purchased on Sai Baba. My name was called so I didn't have to wait before venturing into one of the many treatment rooms.

"Ok you can de robe." Slowly I unclothed soon to realise this wasn't England they meant strip, in no mood to worry about different customs I did just did it, climbing onto the couch that appeared to have snooker pockets I was joined by two male masseurs who begun using large quantities of oil hence the snooker pockets for draining. Now most massages I had experienced usually never quite hit the mark working an area then moving on before I felt the area was finished. As they begun to ring out every ounce of stress I may have been holding in my body I realised this was to be different... By the end I'd forgotten everything, including the nasal treatment I'd signed up for. "Ok Jason you lay your head back, when we hold this nostril, breath deeply through other, yes!"

Physically rung out I laid my head back, a moment later they poured hot oil into my left nostril. Snorting it was horrible but as he continued to pour but there was no time to think. Switching nostrils I began to cough and splutter. "Spit in here." To my side I saw a bucket being lifted, as they continued to alternate the nostrils snot and phlegm began to rise to the point I began to reach, this went on for some time until I felt totally dazed. Washing me down to remove the oil from my massage I clothed and was then led back to the waiting room where I took a seat for a moment.

Aware a European guy was staring, I addressed him. "What are you here for?"

"Nasal treatment, have you been before?" Smiling I got up and headed for the ashram, where I slept. I was woke by a familiar voice, looking up at Emma I tried a faint smile.

"Jimmy tells me you've been asleep all afternoon, you ok?"

"It's my head, feels like my brain has come loose when I move."

"You don't look good."

"I'll be fine, I been plagued all day by old anxieties that you left me again and you're going to go your own way, but as I've laid here I've come to except if that is your path then I have to let you go."

What makes you think that?"

"Something Jayne told me during a kinesiology, that we would not end up together and it's just a feeling I get since we have arrived here."

"Know one can predict what tomorrow brings this isn't like you to pay it this much attention."

"Its because I love you, always have, always will and I'm struggling with the thought of loosing you again, but its ok whatever happens, cause I know it's for the best." Drifting back to sleep I didn't catch Emma's response.

Chapter 17

Making Wishes

Waking up I wondered what parts of the previous day were real or not. As the morning progressed they became clearer. After reading a letter left by Emma things begun to make more sense. The end of the note she asked me if I would meet her after breakfast in the village for a stroll. Walking through to the Bathroom I couldn't believe how clear my head had become. It was as if someone had scrubbed the area around my brain leaving it light sharp and alert. Seeing Jimmy reminded me more of the previous day. "You alright mate?" He asked. "You were out cold for quite some time."

"Yeah feeling great, despite the horrible buzz that nasal Treatment caused, I feel absolutely spot on now I am awake".

The Morning continued with people expressing there concern at me being out cold for Most of the previous day, but my mind was firmly fixed on one thing Emma. The nagging anxiety from the previous day had gone, leaving a sense of light detachment.

Queuing for Darsham I chose line three, sure enough I was called second and placed somewhere almost identically to where I had sat over a year ago. I'd grown since and was now beginning to recognise my true worth, unlike before instead of bowing my head I sat alert while confidently looking for the little man with the big hair do. Entering Sai Baba did his usual round until he was on the home straight and heading my way. Men from all corners of the world excitedly held up letters they had written in the hope that Baba would take theirs. A quick glance in my direction, and he was gone. Despite no interview or chat I felt good that I had kept visual contact the whole time. Confidently I accepted that I had the potential for great deeds of service.

Gulping breakfast rumour soon got round that Baba was leaving for Whitefield another ashram and that thousands were going to follow. Acting quickly I backed those staying and not those preparing for the mass exodus. With so many people on the move I wondered what the female side of the group had decided and went to find Emma. Ten minutes later I had tracked her down. "Jesus this place has gone crazy, what are the Rest of the girls doing?"

"A few decided to leave, but the bulk of us have decided to stay put for a few days, see what happens." Having only just arrived I was in no mood to move so her comments were reassuring. While deciding what to next a series of coincides that would later Snow Ball into an amazing synchronicity begun.

"Hey, the streets are jammed with people." I suddenly said. "How about I take you down to the wish fulfilling tree I told you about? I reckon if we can get down there it will be quiet now."

"Yeah, that would be great." Grabbing her little bag of pencils Emma was ready. Moving into the street we slowly made our way along it...Several minutes later a commotion behind us broke out causing us to stop and look. "Judging by all that activity I reckon that must be Baba leaving."

"Yeah," Emma said "it looks as though his vehicle and the crowd are coming this way."

Pulling Emma by the hand we moved to one side of the road. For a brief moment the wave of people flooding in our direction triggered a panic button, then like the famous parting of the red sea we found ourselves alone next to the car carrying Baba, barely a metre away he smiled at us both before we were once again consumed by the hustle.

Making our way up to the wishing tree, I think we both felt a strange Sense of destiny.

"That was pretty freaky or was it just me?" I finally commented.

"No, the way everything just moved aside was, well incredible. Jay, do you love me?"

Smiling back at Emma I sighed a deep breath.

"Put it this way, I have been pondering over love and what it means. I can get my head around 'no attachment's' as the only true expression of love, as ultimately this is our goal, service through love. Over the last few days I've been tested in this area and been found wanting, it goes back to knowing

137

knowledge and living it. My attachments to you are there, and I can't hide from them, but it seems to have triggered an inner response that love with attachment' is just a path to more hurt and pain, hence the emotions I've been experiencing, but this morning I also recognised I cannot allow this to stop me from trying, as it's only through living without fear that I will progress. So yes I do Love you."

"Jesus I only wanted a yes or no!"

Reaching the tree we sat to admire the fantastic view of the valley, feeling less serious and comfortable we set about discussing all the places we would visit. Smiling I looked at Emma.

"Shall we make a joint wish Em?"

"Ok what will it be?"

"Do ya still want to marry me?"

"Of course."

"Then let's ask for a blessing to marry." I said in a bold playful manner

"Yeah let's do it." Making our wish on a small piece of Emma's note paper we hung them among the many other wishes there. We were in mid sentence when best part of our group and all the friends we had made turned up. As we drifted back through the village with them I found myself talking to Molly an old friend of Jan's who had attended one of Mr Leason's lessons with her. As our conversation unfolded it seemed that Mr Leason had been wrong in his predictions. "Are you telling me the point of evolution I was given, what five years ago could be wrong?"

"Absolutely," Mol continued. "When Mr Crème found out what he'd been doing based on peoples signatures he got a bit of a telling off, as the only person who can give you this is a master. And only then once you have shown a firm understanding of your own ray structure."

"Ah yes the Rays, I have looked at them but they are very subtle in their differences, the idea of a governing energy over each of my vehicles I haven't quite got yet, so in your opinion I would be as well to ignore what Mr Leason told me?"

"Yes." With Molly's conformation a huge sigh of relief came, and the burden of believing I was unevolved dissolved.

Finding ourselves at the end of the village Jimmy gestured that we go into a small temple with him for a blessing with my mood one of flow I had no objections.

As we moved about underneath the low roof a kind looking man began to individually bless us, it was a warm feeling capping a good morning.

Walking back to the ashram Vishal made a beeline for me. "I see you and your lady friend made a wish together?"

"Well, we are a couple." Emma said.

"You are partners yes, very nice and what was your wish?"

"I thought if you told others," Emma continued, "that it took away the energy of the wish."

"Maybe telling someone, the universe can hear you more clearly."

"Ok we asked for a blessing to marry."

"Oh I see, so you wish to marry in Puttaparti with Swami's blessing?"

I laughed at Vishals comment. "That would be something, no just to marry some time in the future, besides we'll be gone in a few days."

"You never know my friend, you never know." Feeling slightly tired I excused myself and went back to the dorm. Ahead of me Jimmy was already having a sort out. "You seen all this stuff, Ray has bought there's mops, buckets and cleaning fluids how long does this guy plan on staying?" Jimmy's bewilderment became a quick source of amusement to me.

"Who knows such things" I said falling onto the bed for a nap. I was in the middle of a strange dream in which my brother was attacked by a wild bear. Whilst trying to save him it turned on me and chewed my arm. Facing death, a voice told me to use the light, imagining light the bear withdrew, focusing light on my mangled arm it instantly healed I was just helping my brother when I was abruptly woken by Vishal. "Jason, Jason sorry to wake you but I have news about your wedding".

"Wedding,"

"Yes I speak to the man at the office he wants to see you, he tell me it is possible."

"You are joking right?"

"Come and see for yourself."

If anything Vishal had me curious. Following Vishal took me to a small side office tucked away behind one of the stores on site.

"This." Vishal said addressing an Indian shuffling some papers is the young man I've been telling you about."

"Come in sit." The Indians brash manor was a little off putting at first.

"So why you want to marry here, you can go home and marry no? We cannot perform your traditional ceremony here, hmm."

"He is happy for traditional Hindu wedding." Vishals comment caught me completely off guard.

"But if he marry this way." The Indian continued. "It will not be legal when he returns home so why you wish to marry?" He turned from Vishal back to me.

"Well the legal bits not important to me, if it were possible it would be more a spiritual experience."

"Yes he is right." Vishal commented.

"I still do not understand but if it means something to you then my brother in the village will help you." Smiling for the first time the Indian looked back at his paper work. Leaving the office vishal told me he would contact me later about the man in the village. Could it be possible I thought.

Returning to my dorm I told Jimmy about it all. "Great but you've only four days as we've decided to leave Monday morning. Have you asked Emma what she thinks about it all?" 'Emma' I thought it had all been such a rush.

Leaving the dorm I tracked her down in one of the many gardens. Commenting on a drawing she was doing I got straight to the point.

"You know we made that wish this morning, well how do you fancy it, here in Puttaparti?"

"You what, you are joking."

"No Vishal thinks it could be possible." Sitting down I relayed to her the events that had taken place that morning. "So what do you think, it'll be an adventure if it's possible, which given the time span I think highly unlikely but just in case I thought I'd best ask being as you are the bride."

"If your game, I am," was her wonderful response.

I didn't see vishal until the next morning catching him up I hid my excitement. "Did you find the man in the village?"

"No, but I will try again today my friend, tell me about you and Emma have you known each other long in this life time?" His comments made me smile. "Oh we know each other pretty well, we met when my family moved up from London I was only nine and she lived two doors down from mine. That first summer of 83, I was instantly drawn to her she was part of a group of kids I grew up with in that street. Every time I asked her out she'd smile and say loose some weight fat boy, not that I was fat. Anyway this went on till I was twelve going on thirteen when the group we'd grown up with began to move away or find other friends. Then one day over the field a lad I was playing with noticed her and commented like most of them did, I mean she was the cutest girl on the block. I told him he'd no chance, she went out with nobody, so he called out gaining her attention. My mate here wants to go out with you; as usual she just smiled and carried on by. Later that day as I drifted back home she was sat on the front door step. Expecting no more than a hello I just smiled at her. Then she asked me if I really did want to go out with her, thinking it was just a wind up given the times I had already asked, I just said 'you know I do.'

"Ok meet me tomorrow." I can still remember the next night, out back after school, I felt like a king meeting his future queen, that's when we had our first kiss. " Pausing I pondered the moment.

"So you have been together since?"

"Oh no, well we did go out with one another for a further six years, but I suppose I allowed my later teen years to shroud my judgement, with an ego like mine and the constant need for approval it took its toll and we split up. We didn't see each other for a further six years, well not, until this summer".

"So she is the one then?"

"Oh yeah, I won't make the same mistakes again I promise you that."

"This is very hard burden you put on yourself with this promise, you would not be human if you not make mistakes my friend."

Vishals comment just fell on death ears, older and more experienced I arrogantly passed off his comment.

That night Jimmy invited us to meet an older couple with a remarkable story.

"Where are they from?" I asked him as we hurried across the Ashram.

"Their American I think that's what David said."
Mmm, and he didn't say what it's about?"
"Just flow with it." Jimmy laughed. Arriving in a crowded room, an old biblical looking couple had already started telling the story. "Now tell them about your experiences with Jesus." David suggested. "Ok." The woman said. "We are living in Detroit where every day I meditate and take advice from my higher self. This day it tells me to say yes to everything, around mid day a voice in my head tells me to prepare a large meal. At first I'm unsure, as it's only my husband coming home that night but I say yes and do it anyway. That afternoon it starts to rain hard becoming dark outside. Then I hear a knock at the door, opening it I see a dark skinned stranger, weathered with a beard he stands next to a motor bike. I ask him what he wants, he tells me he has come for the meal I am preparing. At first I'm a little scared as this is Detroit, but I remember my higher self and look into his eyes and see a deep passive soul, and so invite him in. He then tells me to invite over the rest of my family for the meal, and goes into the bathroom. I continue with the meal until my husband returns, I tell him about my day and the stranger in our bathroom, of course he is concerned but he trusts me. Three hours later most of our family have arrived but the man is still in the bathroom, so I knock, and to my surprise the man appears only this time clean and smart, he comes and joins us at the table, of course everyone is curious. Then he starts to tell us a little about each of us, things only we could know. Then I

144

realise he is not an ordinary man but a master. In total he stayed with us three days, where upon leaving we finally realised he is the master Jesus" My initial thought was inspiring, there was not a shed of untruth in her voice. They went onto express other amazing meetings and story's, I sat transfixed, on what turned out to be a fascinating night, my mind had begun to wonder even before I left the room imagining meeting and speaking with masters coupled with miracles I slept well that night.

Chapter 18

Dreams

Friday morning arrived and Vishal hadn't got back to me, nor had Baba returned.

We found ourselves once again in a group, wandering through the village to pass time we got to know another better than before. It was while sat drinking outside one of the many coffee shops that Vishal turned up.

"Jason there you are, I have news, the village priest he will meet you tonight at eight o'clock." Of course all those present wanted to know what he was on about. Attempting to answer and listen at the same time became almost humorous; everyone seemed so excited about the idea.

"Surely time is against us now?" I expressed to Vishal beneath raised eyebrows.

"You should never doubt Swami, Miracles happen here." Vishals optimism gave me new hope, but also left me with a nagging anxiety what was I thinking, weddings don't happen over night and what about family, shit I hadn't even thought about them. Was I in my ego right now caught in the glamour of some crazy fantasy about a spiritual wedding? Accepting what will be, will be time alone in the meditation garden brought some clarity.

That evening after what appeared to be a long day, me, Jimmy Vishal and Ray set off into the village stopping outside a silk shop Vishal smiled. "We wait here for man to take us." Being as it was already eight, I began to doubt again. I had told Emma just in case to get measured for a sari with the idea if it didn't happen it would make nice keep sake anyway. After ten or twelve minutes Vishal became anxious. "I will go see where my friend is."

While he disappeared into the busy street I quietly closed my eyes and drew breath, savouring the familiar scents that could be caught floating around, some were sweet, others smelly but it was India always changing, moving and flowing.

Reappearing from the crowd Vishal puffed. "I don't understand he assured me he would be here."

With the ashram gates due to be closed at nine I resigned myself to put the crazy dream to bed and head back.

"Why don't we go visit the priest ourselves?"

"That's just it Ray." I said. "I don't think anyone here knows who he is."

"He is the man who gave you blessing the other day in little temple."

"Are you sure" I asked.

"Yes."

Getting up Jimmy threw his arms in the air. "You mean we been stood here all this time and you knew who it was all along?"

"No one asked." Bewildered Ray shrugged. Like some scene from an old movie Jimmy wasted no time getting up and flagging down an old rick shack. Weaving through the crazy streets a crazed over flow of laughter ensued. Pulling up outside the tiny temple we'd previously visited the very same priest as if expecting us was sat outside as we approached. One of the waiting flower girls asked if she could be of assistance, so I explained to her why we were there. The young girl who spoke good English began to translate our intentions to the priest.

"He tells me you need to give him both birthdates as this will help determined when you can marry." Surely we ain't come this far for him to tell me in the spring I thought. Writing the dates down I watched carefully as he performed some sort of ritual over the birthdates.

"Yes." He tells me you can marry here tomorrow at two o'clock." At first the young girls comment didn't register.

"Oh my, I knew swami would make it happen." Vishals excitement was contagious. "Congratulations." Shaking my hand Ray beamed from ear to ear.

My own mind was now whizzing, Rings, outfits, I knew nothing about Hindu customs and for a moment I became oblivious to where I was.

"I can help you." The young flower girl said, but before I could answer Vishal was saying the same thing.

"This young lady is happy to help you with preparations and the priest requires two thousand rupees for the ceremony. Oh and you will need a sacred necklace of some sort as well as rings."

"Sacred necklace what does that mean?"

"Just a stone or something you can give to your wife to be."

I began to laugh at the synchronicity that was unfolding.

"What do you find so humorous, young man?"

"The pearl, she kept it all those years and now wears it around her neck after I had it set in gold for her birthday."

"This is wonderful." Vishal responded.

The young flower girl explained how she could arrange flowers from Bangalore, a six man band and a shave at the local barbers in the morning. Savouring the unfolding miracle I sat peacefully for a moment.

"We got plenty of time don't worry mate it will be fun sorting it out tomorrow." Jimmy was a master at being laid back and his timely words reassured me. Going back to the ashram that night I was amazed at how things were rolling, it really was going to happen.

Lying in bed I began to ponder what this meant to me. Emma during our years apart had become this inspirational figure, she was a rare diamond, on the surface she still had issues, but in that heart was the rarest of love, devotional and pure unspoilt by toxins, or soured by life. The innocence of a child creating perfumes from her mother's roses, a seeker of truth, someone who trusted the world, with the richest of souls. She was the light that inspired me to be a better person, to fight the good fight to my last breath, and if the whole world turned to darkness, I would stand alone with the light in my heart to defend the rarest of diamonds because that's how she made me feel. Because of this I knew my ego was ready and willing to destroy my heart or Emma's, and this ultimately would be my greatest challenge. A cold fear washed over me as if I was being reminded of my own mortality, my heart is strong was my thought, but so is my Ego. Fighting inner battles my mind eventually drifted to Lancelot the brave knight, the man who couldn't separate the love of his king and queen, or betray his oath, yet when his king found himself out numbered and nearly defeated, Lancelot found salvation by fighting the good fight one last time beside his king. I reminded myself that however my Ego influenced my life I had nothing to fear for in my heart I'd discovered peace, faith, service, love and light reminding me of my true self. I was about to embark on one of my greatest journeys, so I affirmed to myself, 'feel the fear and do it anyway.'

With this in mind my energies began to rise. So imagining myself like the great knight, El cid riding through the gates of destiny, my inner child soured and all my boyhood heroes, merged then dissipated leaving just this beautiful radiant child that was me. Knowing I would never surrender this child like essence left me in no doubt that life is the most amazing, precious journey any soul can take.

The next day is best summed up with an old saying me mum would always use.

"A little bit of faith and we can move mountains."

The friends I was with alongside the people of Putter parti showed me that there is no division in family, we are all one. And to Emma who on the 5th of December at two o'clock proved to me that dreams can come true.

Epilogue

Our wedding day was everything it promised to be, dream like, romantic and spontaneous. We enjoyed the next five months travelling before returning to England. My decision to quit smoking altogether was successful and to date I have enjoyed a smoke free existence. Despite my early reservations of ever enjoying a meat free diet, I never went back to meat after those chicken portions my friend Nat fed me when I arrived back from India. There have been other life changing decisions that have worked out, but without the help the universe has given me it is my belief I would have continued to look outside myself for peace and answers. I went on to eventually complete my Reiki masters, teaching locally through the adult education system as well as privately, along with meditation for modern living. I am still actively asking the universe for help in all that I do, and continue to be amazed by the answers that flow through me and around me. We were blessed with a beautiful daughter the year after India and have done our best to continue with life's flow. Professionally after years of struggle and training, I now run a successful tree surgery business. Privately I have continued to paint with oils, exhibiting locally on numerous occasions and hope to have an exhibition with Emma sometime soon. Throughout it all I learned to honour the inner child that resides in us all, never surrender for life is a miracle. Enjoy it.

Printed in the United Kingdom
by Lightning Source UK Ltd.
128058UK00001B/13-30/P